HEGEL'S EDUCATIONAL THEORY AND PRACTICE

BY

MILLICENT MACKENZIE, M.A.

Professor of Education, University College, Cardiff

WITH AN INTRODUCTORY NOTE BY

J. S. MACKENZIE, LITT.D.

Professor of Philosophy, University College, Cardiff

GREENWOOD PRESS, PUBLISHERS
WESTPORT, CONNECTICUT

Originally published in 1909
by Swan Sonnenschein & Co., Ltd., London

Reprinted from an original copy in the collections
of the Brooklyn Public Library

First Greenwood Reprinting 1970

Library of Congress Catalogue Card Number 77-109973

SBN 8371-4478-7

Printed in the United States of America

TO
C. E. H.

PREFACE

This little book aims at bringing the educational views and work of Hegel under the notice of teachers and of others who believe that philosophy has a direct bearing upon life and education. The Hegelian point of view in education has hitherto been almost entirely neglected in this country in favour of philosophic positions which are utilitarian or realistic in character. There are, however, unmistakable signs of a growing demand for a more idealistic interpretation of education, and these pages are offered to students of the subject in the hope of stimulating further investigation into the value of the Hegelian philosophy as a basis for educational theory and practice.

In the United States Dr Harris led the way in emphasising the importance of Hegel in relation to education, and Dr .Lurqueer, of Columbia University, whose book, "Hegel as Educator," only came under my notice after my own was written, has still further helped to make Hegel available for students, by translating under the above title the most important parts of Von Thaulow's "Hegel's Ansichten."

References to passages in Hegel's writings are always made to the collected edition of his works published in 1840

Llanishen,
Nr. Cardiff.

TABLE OF CONTENTS

PART II

CONTRIBUTIONS TO THEORY OF EDUCATION

INTRODUCTORY NOTE

THE saying of Hegel has often been quoted, that the penalty which a great man inflicts upon the world is to force it to explain him. Certainly in few cases has this penalty been so heavy as in Hegel's own. For several generations and in many lands—assuredly not least in ours—the attempt to understand him has been pursued with vigour ; and still there are very few who could venture to affirm that they have grasped his significance. We are only slowly, and bit by bit, arriving at a proper appreciation of his place in the world of thought and action, and of the many aspects in which his work may be viewed.

Of all the aspects of his work, it can hardly be doubted that the educational side is the one to which least attention has been given in this country. Few realise how large a part of his time and energy was given up to the teaching of the young and to the organisation of their studies, and how well, on the whole, his genius was adapted for work of this kind. It is of course true that this aspect of his life has not so obvious a dominance as it has in the case of Herbart. But they both lived in an age and country in which the schoolmaster was very emphatically finding his place. The call of Rousseau had been heard throughout Europe ; and Germany, in particular, had woke up to the great task of reconstructing its national life ; and had entered upon it with an enthusiasm like that which, in more recent times, has

been at work in Japan. In this great work Hegel was
undoubtedly one of the chief formative influences. It
was his aim throughout to make philosophy in the fullest
sense German, and to make Germany in the best sense
philosophic ; and it can hardly be denied that he was
very largely successful in both directions. At any rate,
we cannot hope to understand rightly the nature of his
work unless we constantly bear in mind that he was not
only seeking to discover the truth but also to teach it and
make it generally accessible.

It may thus pretty safely be said that the educational
aspect of his work was constantly present to his mind.
This is no doubt in some degree true of all philosophical
writers. But it is hardly an exaggeration to say that the
Hegelian philosophy is in its essence educational in a way
that no other philosophy is, with the single exception of
that of Plato. What I mean is that these two philosophers are constantly endeavouring to see, not merely—
like all other philosophers—what the truth is, but also
how it is to be reached and appropriated by a mind to
which it is naturally remote and foreign ; and they both
believe that the process by which this is to be done is
dialectical. There is, indeed, a difference between the
two in this respect ; and it may be said of Hegel, in
contrast with Plato, that it is the education of the race,
rather than that of the individual, that he has continu-
ally in his mind. It is the human mind, rather than the
mind of the pupil, in the development of which he is
primarily interested. But, after all this is not a very
important difference ; for it is one of his most fundamental convictions, that the individual must on the whole
go through the very same process for his development as
that which is necessary for the development of the race.

Hence, in tracing the movement of thought by which the world is growing, he believes himself to be at the same time bringing out the process by which the individual must unfold what is contained within himself. In this conviction I suppose most of our recent psychologists would in the main concur with him ; though they might not all admit that Hegel had been quite successful in tracing the process. It is not improbable that his interpretation of it was a little too rigid in its outlines.

If the view here taken is correct, it is evident that the study of Hegel's attitude towards education is important, not only from its intrinsic interest and value, but also for the light that it throws upon his philosophy as a whole. In the present work an effort is made to bring out both its philosophical significance and its practical bearings. I believe that such an attempt ought to be specially useful to English readers at the present time. The general conceptions with which Hegel works have now gained a considerable degree of currency among us ; and it has become a good deal easier than it once was to appreciate fresh aspects of his thought. In particular, the issue of a translation of the *Phänomenologie* (written at the time when he was most actively engaged in teaching) ought to be a great help to the understanding of the educational side of his philosophy.

Hegel is so very German, that anything he said or did (however careful one may be in translating, adapting and explaining) is sure to seem at first somewhat foreign, and even somewhat repellent, to most English readers. With regard to his educational work, in particular, there are some objections that are pretty certain to occur to the minds of many ; and, without making any attempt to give an exhaustive statement of such objections, or in any thorough way to meet them, it may be worth while to notice here one or two of the most prominent of them.

1. Some will be apt to think that they see traces of the Prussian drill sergeant in some of Hegel's methods. It may even be urged that, just as Plato had rather too exclusively in his mind the preparation of those who were to be rulers in his State, and especially the training that is necessary for the production of the 'philosopher-king,' so Hegel has too much in his mind the education that is wanted for a State official. How would his methods apply, we are tempted to inquire, to the education of engineers, stockbrokers, or tradesmen, or again to the education of girls ? A partial answer may be given, I think, by bearing in mind that Hegel's special problem was the organisation of secondary education, and especially of the kind of training that prepares for the work of the university. But a thorough treatment of this particular problem can hardly fail to throw light on other aspects of education as well. A more adequate answer, however, may be suggested by one of the sayings of T. H. Green, who, if not quite in the strictest sense a Hegelian, was certainly one of those who most fully caught the best spirit of Hegel's teaching. In one of his educational addresses, delivered to the new Oxford High School for Boys, Green concludes with this general remark : " Our High School may fairly claim to be helping forward the time when every Oxford citizen will have open to him at least the precious companionship of the best books in his own language, and the knowledge necessary to make him really independent ; when all who have a special taste for learning will have open to them what has hitherto been unpleasantly called the ' education of gentlemen.' I confess to hoping for a time when that phrase will have

lost its meaning, because the sort of education which alone makes the gentleman in any true sense will be within the reach of all. As it was the aspiration of Moses that all the Lord's people should be prophets, so with all serious-ness and reverence we may hope and pray for a condition of English society in which all honest citizens will recog-nise themselves and be recognised by each other as gentle-men." This passage seems to me to be a very good ' translation into English ' of the spirit by which Hegel was animated. His primary aim was not that of making State officials or ' philosopher - kings,' any more than engineers or stockbrokers, but rather that of making good citizens. And I think we are gradually coming to see that this is at bottom the chief aim of all real educa-tion—and that for girls as well as for boys.

2. It may be urged, again, that Hegel is too purely a Humanist ; that he emphasises mainly the importance of historical and literary studies, and does not sufficiently bring out the value of the natural sciences. But, if there is any truth in this, we may at least answer once more that this is not a kind of one-sidedness by which we are at present in much danger of being misled. We have Herbert Spencer always with us to keep the claims of the sciences in our minds ; and the danger is on the whole, at the present time, that these claims may be somewhat over-pressed. It is the utilitarian value of scientific studies that is usually most prominent in men's minds. Now, in a sense, Hegel's view of education was thoroughly utilitarian. Like Plato, he believed most emphatically that all education is with a view to life ; but I think they would both have added—what the modern mind is not always so ready to grant—that all life is with a view to education. They thought that to make good men and

good citizens is the first of all aims of education ; and
that to make skilled workers in particular departments,
though important, is only the second aim.   I believe we
ought to think many times before we decide that they
were wrong.   It should be remembered, moreover, that
if Hegel was a Humanist, he was, at any rate, a scientific
Humanist.   He was not primarily a grammarian or
philologist in his teaching work, but rather one who
sought to bring out the bearings of history and literature
on the problems of our present life.

3. Another kind of objection that may be raised
(though for this, at least, there is extremely little foundation) is to the effect that Hegel does not sufficiently
emphasise the imaginative, or at least the emotional,
aspects of education, as against the more strictly intellectual.   Here again, in so far as there is any truth in the
suggestion, a partial answer may be given by saying that
these aspects had been a good deal over-emphasised by
Rousseau and some of his disciples, and that Hegel
represents a very necessary reaction against such excess.
It should be remembered also that he regards the teaching
of the school as supplementary to that of the home, in
which the emotional element would naturally have a
larger place.

We in this country, with our rich poetic literature and
our traditions of classical study, are not on the whole
in any great danger of forgetting the value of imaginative and emotional culture.   In particular, we have
Wordsworth's educational writings as a constant reminder.
And indeed, if we study what Wordsworth has to say, we
shall find, I believe, that his teaching is very largely in
harmony with that of Hegel.   He sought in ' Nature '
for that ' self-estrangement ' and self-recovery which

Hegel preferred to find in the literature and history of the Greeks and Romans ; and he expresses himself in the language of feeling and imagination, rather than in that of logical analysis. But the essential meaning of the two writers is very largely the same. Indeed, it is hardly an exaggeration to say in general that our English poets have all along been teaching us in their way what the German philosophers have sought to express in theirs. The language of the spirit has these two voices, the poetic and the logical ; and no doubt we have need of both. But it can at least not be maintained by anyone that Hegel did not sufficiently bring out the importance of the appreciation of the beautiful in the education of the young. It is the one thing about which he is specially enthusiastic.

4. Again, it may be objected (and this is, at least, more plausible) that in his educational views, as in other aspects of his philosophy, Hegel did not lay enough emphasis upon the cultivation of the will, and in general upon the importance of human individuality. If there is any truth in this objection, it is probably to a large extent a defect that he shares with Herbart. But again, one has always to remember that Hegel has in his mind the prevailing tendency to over-emphasise the side of action, as against that of thought. Kant and Fichte, for instance, had both rather tended in this direction. And certainly in this country at the present time, with the exuberant William James as our most influential psychologist, and with all his hosts of Pragmatists at his heels—not to mention the more cautious volitionism of James Ward, Josiah Royce, G. F. Stout, and, in another language, the rising power of Bergson—we are not very likely to forget this aspect of life and education.

' Efficiency ' is indeed the watchword of our age. Nor
are we likely to overlook—what is closely connected with
the same point—the value of play, and in general the
importance of spontaneity, as opposed to drill. I may
admit, however, that, if Hegel's educational teaching has
any real defect, it is probably to be sought mainly on this
side. Though eminently practical, he had always the
underlying conviction that any genuine efficiency must
rest on profound insight ; and it may be that, like
Socrates, he over-emphasised this truth.

But on the whole I venture to claim for Hegel, that he
supplies us more than any other educator (more even
than Herbart, because his educational ideas are based
upon a deeper philosophy) with just those things that we
are most in want of in our time and country. The
defects to which I have alluded, if they are real at all,
would certainly be found, on careful consideration, to be
much slighter than at first appears ; and it would be
found, nearly always, that he lays the emphasis on the
most important points. There is a ripe wisdom in most
of his utterances. One feels that they are based on keen
observation, as well as on careful reflection. Especially
when the great problem of moral and civic education is
coming more and more prominently to the front, we may
hope to find in him one of our safest guides. The magni-
ficent example of Japan has shown us how much may be
accomplished by this kind of education ; and it is on this
side—on the making of the good man and citizen—that
Hegel throws most light.

It may be added also that the consideration of Hegel's
educational aims and methods enables us to understand
his life and personality more fully than we can from
his more purely philosophical writings. Although the

general ideas contained in these are now pretty widely known, Hegel has certainly not yet become, for most people in this country, so vivid a reality in himself as Kant and Schopenhauer—hardly even as Leibnitz, Fichte and Nietzsche. Yet surely he was quite as remarkable a man as any of them. And it is still true that to understand a man's philosophy it is almost necessary in some degree to realise his personality. For a man's philosophy, when it is genuinely his own, is a summing up of the experience of his life, and the expression of its inmost meaning.

These remarks have been suggested to me by reading this little book ; and perhaps they may help to bring out its significance for some other readers.

J. S. MACKENZIE.

UNIVERSITY COLLEGE,
    CARDIFF.

Hegel's Educational Theory and Practice

PART I

LIFE OF HEGEL

WITH SPECIAL REFERENCE TO HIS EARLY EDUCATION
AND CAREER AS SCHOOLMASTER

CHAPTER I

YOUTH AND EDUCATION

IN considering the life of Hegel from the point of view of
his connection with education, it is obvious that there are
at least two periods which it will be desirable to study
with special attention—viz., the period of his youth,
when he was himself in the making ; and the period of
his active work as a teacher of boys and Rector of the
Nürnberg Gymnasium. Other periods of his life and
aspects of his work may be of greater general interest and
value, but for our purpose the above-mentioned have
special significance, and although it will be both impossible
and undesirable to isolate them completely from the rest
of his life, yet it is to these in particular that we shall
mainly confine our attention.

A   I

The relation between a teacher's own early education and his subsequent practical work in his profession is sufficiently obvious.

It might even be said that most people have been through at least one course of training for the work of teaching—that, namely, of their own early education, when indeed they tested methods of instruction and discipline in a very direct manner and gained much practical even if one-sided experience of their efficacy or inadequacy. No doubt this experience is chiefly of value as material for reflection in later life, when it can be studied in the light of philosophy and educational science ; still all thoughtful teachers will acknowledge that much in a professional training course, and in subsequent teaching work, receives point and value from the memories of their own home and school education, and would be almost unintelligible without such a background of experience.

Indeed we may go further, and say that it is just this element of personal experience, coloured by natural temperament, that gives to a teacher's work its force, freshness and originality. The subjects which quickened our own minds in youth, by means of which we first realised the higher life of thought, of goodness, of beauty, are those in which as teachers we shall have faith. Without that inner spring of belief in the value of the subjects taught, instruction becomes lifeless and ineffective.

It does not, of course, always follow that our school studies were those which stirred us thus, indeed it is possible for a pupil to pass through school (and even the university) before finding what he needs.

There are those to whom language and even literature make but slight appeal, and who owe their first awakening of intellectual life to some scientific study carried on outside the school, or even perhaps not begun until ordinary schooldays were past ; or a pupil brought up on science may starve for lack of that suitable nourishment which he might have assimilated from history or literature. When, however, the pupil does find in the subjects he studies at school those best suited to his needs, he will be likely not only to have faith in them, but also in his teacher's methods.

Hegel was happy in that his schooldays brought him what he needed, subjects and methods congenial to his type of mind, and at least one master whose memory was cherished as that of an almost ideal teacher.

Hegel has himself told us, that there are *five* instruments of education—viz., the family, the school, rank or social class, people or nation, the Church ; and the influence of all these is clearly to be traced in his own life and character.

Georg Wilhelm Friedrich Hegel was born at Stuttgart in Würtemberg on 27th August 1770. His father was a secretary in the revenue office, a highly respected man of business, by whose example, no doubt, he was encouraged to form those habits of regular, orderly work and attention to detail which contributed in no small degree to his subsequent success, both as teacher and headmaster.

His mother seems to have been a woman of taste and refinement. She was his first teacher, and although he passed from under her direct instruction at an early age, her interest in his school studies and intellectual development must have been a valuable stimulus to his progress.

Her death, when he was only thirteen, was a great blow to him, and its sobering influence at a most impressionable age may account in some measure for the somewhat precocious gravity and earnestness with which he pursued his studies.

He had one brother, Louis, younger than himself, and one sister, Christiane. Between him and his sister there was much in common, and their friendship was lifelong. Brought up thus, in a quiet, middle-class family, with its placid round of work, and simple interests, its atmoshpere of affection, its freedom alike from the grinding care of poverty and the distractions of wealth, the boy had leisure and opportunity to develop normally, and to lay the foundations of a strong, steadfast character and solid intellectual interests.

As regards his nationality, it is not enough merely to say that he was a German, for, as is well known, that nation includes many different types of people. A native of Stuttgart, the capital of Würtemberg, he belonged by race to the Swabians, who yet hold to Protestantism, the northern form of religion.

It has been well said that " in the general character- istics " they " form a sort of middle term between the different branches of the German nation." " The hard rationalism and practical energy which distinguishes the Protestant North, and especially Prussia, is in them softened and widened by what the German calls the

Gemüthlichkeit of a southern race, and has given rise to a certain meditative depth of nature." [1]

In Hegel all these different characteristics meet, and must be taken account of by those who would really understand him. He is the practical, hard-working teacher and civil servant ; while at the same time he is the idealistic philosopher, living apparently on the intellectual plane alone. On the one hand he is the severe logical reasoner, disdaining all vagueness and "picture thinking," on the other—though possibly unrealised by himself—we find him intuitional, and even mystical.

It is doubtless this duality in his nature that has caused him to be so much misunderstood and misrepresented.

Indeed it is not easy to relate him, on the one hand with the somewhat rigid, Prussian school code, and on the other with the mystical views of Boehme. Yet it is clear that in Prussia Hegel was regarded as the champion of orthodoxy, conservatism, law and order, that his philosophy was the recognised State philosophy—a guarantee of political and social soundness—while in Great Britain and elsewhere there has been a tendency to regard it as subversive of religious orthodoxy and indicative of the wildest and most unprofitable speculations.

In truth there meet in him many opposites which he sought, with more or less success, to reconcile, but of those who read his writings some are not at all desirous of such reconciliation, and they either ignore one side or the other or are repelled by any attempt to bring together

[1] "Hegel," by Edward Caird.

those characteristics which they regard as separated from each other by their very nature.

But perhaps what these opposing tendencies in Hegel's life and character really emphasise is — that he was very *human*. No fact comes out more clearly in the biographies of great men (and the same would be true of lesser men too) than that each has at least "two soul sides," and often many more.

Hegel's reputation has to some extent suffered through the fact that he has been regarded, in this country at least, almost entirely as the abstruse philosopher. What we shall now attempt to show is that he was also a practical man, in the best sense of the word—one capable both of formulating his ideas and of carrying them out successfully; one who lived neither in the world of the past, attractive as it ever was to him ; nor in the world of the future, firm believer as he was in evolution and the progress of life, but one who lived in the present world and, in spite of all its shortcomings, found it good to be here.

At the age of five he was sent to school, a so-called Latin school, which he left two years later to enter the Stuttgart Gymnasium, where he remained as a pupil for ten years (1777-1787). His school record was one of uninterrupted progress. He showed no early signs of originality, but an unusual power of orderly intellectual assimilation. School work was congenial to him, and he was fortunate in having as form master for the first two years of his school life one who understood and encouraged him. This master, Löffler by name, appears to have been a man of wide interests and culture, and to have exercised considerable influence over his pupils.

He had the happy knack of making them feel that his teaching work was not mere duty, but a real joy to him. In the little Wilhelm Hegel he recognised signs of great promise, and continued to show interest in the boy even when no longer his form master. When higher up in the school, Hegel had coaching lessons from Löffler, sometimes with other boys and sometimes alone.

It is pleasant to learn that it was to him that Hegel owed his first introduction to the works of Shakespeare. Löffler presented him, when only eight years of age, with a copy of Wieland's translation of Shakespeare, saying : " You will not understand it now, but you will soon learn to understand it." Little Wilhelm, we are told, forthwith began his Shakespearean studies by reading *The Merry Wives of Windsor*.

Löffler died in 1785, and Hegel records, in the diary, which he had just begun to keep, his deep sense of what he owed to this revered teacher. He writes thus :

" His chief care was to be of use to his pupils, and to the world." " He knew the value of knowledge and the consolation it ensures in the midst of life's uncertainties." " How often and how contentedly did he sit by me, and I by him in that beloved little room." [1] " Few knew his true worth. Now he has fallen asleep, but ever shall I bear his memory in my heart."

The course of study pursued at the Stuttgart Gymnasium was almost entirely linguistic and literary. Latin, Greek and a little Hebrew, French and Mathematics were included in the curriculum.

[1] During the coaching lessons above referred to.

Special attention was given to the study of the classics, and Hegel appears to have acquired a good reading acquaintance with the chief poets, historians and philosophers of antiquity.

History had a peculiar attraction for him, and he was fond of trying to sum up for himself the chief characteristics of different nations. It is in reference to this taste that Rosenkranz refers to him as "a poly-historian while at the gymnasium."

He became also much absorbed in Greek literature. The "Antigone" in particular made a deep and lasting impression upon him. He regarded it as the most perfect expression of the real Greek spirit, and in his enthusiasm even attempted a translation. There is ample evidence of wide reading on his part, especially during the last two or three years of his school life.

Reference has already been made to his diary, carefully kept from 1785 to 1787, and written partly in German and partly in Latin. In it he records the course of his reading, and adds such comments and criticisms as show that he was already beginning to reflect on the fundamental problems of life. He criticises the methods of study then in vogue and urges in particular that in the study of Latin too much attention is given to language —to words and phrases—too little to the literature and thought.

Besides the diary, he also kept commonplace books, into which he copied impressive passages from the writings of those authors he was reading, and also extracts from books dealing with topics which interested him, and which he wished to preserve for future reference.

These were all written on separate sheets of paper, lettered, indexed, and carefully kept in portfolios or sliding cases labelled according to subject. From these we gather that even while at school his reading covered a wide range of subjects—Literature, History, Philology, Mathematics, Physics, Pedagogy, Travels, Philosophy, etc., are all included. It is interesting to note that this habit of making extracts, formed during his school days, remained with him through life.

His pocket money seems to have been largely spent in the purchase of books, and he evidently took great pride in his gradually increasing library. He kept a catalogue of his books, and each addition was made to it under the following headings : 1. Title. 2. Edition. 3. Place and date of publication. 4. Price paid. Several of his most treasured books were purchased when the library of his former master, Löffler, was put up to auction.

Of the influence of contemporary literature upon him there is no trace, and it seems probable that, during his school years at least, the works of Lessing, Goethe and other German writers were practically unknown to him. Yet from his diary we learn, almost with relief, of one lapse from the usual severity of his course of reading. On the 1st January 1789 he records the fact that he had not done several things he had intended to do— because he was reading a novel, and could not lay it down.[1]

In the higher classes of the gymnasium it was customary to require each pupil to compose and deliver a short lecture or address in German at least once a year.

[1] "Sophien's Reise von Memel nach Sachsen," by J. T. Hermes.

Hegel appears to have given four of these, including his valedictory address on leaving the gymnasium.

The pupils were apparently left quite free in regard to choice of subject and mode of treatment, but they were afterwards very carefully criticised as to their performance — matter, style, and delivery all being taken into account. In the case of Hegel the content, style and arrangement of his discourse seem to have been invariably commended — not so, however, his delivery. He was not a born orator, and his lack of fluency and ease as a speaker was very marked, and this defect remained with him more or less through life.

The subjects he chose indicate to some extent the development of his studies and interests. His first address, delivered on 31st May 1785, was entitled " Conversation on the Subject of the Triumvirate between Antony, Octavius and Lepidus." The second (10th August 1787) dealt with the religious ideas of the Greeks and Romans. The third (7th August 1788) treated of " Some Characteristic Differences between Ancient and Modern Poets." His fourth and last subject was : " The Unfortunate Condition of the Arts and Sciences amongst the Turks." The choice of this difficult and somewhat unusual subject for treatment by a schoolboy indicates that he was approaching maturity and ready to take part in dealing with the problems of the day. In this address he first formulates his views as to the importance of a good system of education in promoting the development of a State. He attributes the terrible condition of Turkey largely to its neglect of education. As this

was really his farewell speech to his school, he concludes with a grateful reference to the excellent provision
made for education in his own native state and town,
and especially in the much-loved gymnasium where so
many happy years of his life had been spent.

It is not without significance that these subjects, in
the order of choice, indicate to some extent the path
along which, according to his later educational views,
Hegel believed the mind must be developed. This
point will be more fully discussed elsewhere, and here
it must suffice to point out that he regarded the step of
" self-estrangement " as being necessary to progress.
In education this step, he believed, could best be secured
by helping the pupils to become absorbed in the life of
classical times. They are to become, for the time,
Greeks and Romans, removed in thought completely
from the life of their own day. In choosing his first
subject Hegel showed that he had indeed taken that step
and was able to identify himself with the personalities
and interests of the classic age.

After self - estrangement comes the gradual return
journey of the mind to itself—a process of disentangling,
abstracting, generalising, comparing and reconciling.
This part of the process is suggested by the next two
subjects chosen. He has so far withdrawn himself from
the Greeks and Romans that he is able to reflect and
generalise upon their religious views. A still further
step is taken when he attempts to bring the ancients
and moderns into relation with each other on the
common ground of poetry, while yet clearly differentiating between them.

The step which finally indicates at least some measure of mental maturity is taken when the mind, enriched with the gains of its harvest in foreign lands, enters into full possession of itself, realises its own powers and attempts to cope with the life and problems of its own day and with its own individual experience. It may be that the choice of a present - day problem, like the condition of Turkey, implied that Hegel had begun to realise that he had entered into his own kingdom, and would henceforth think for himself, and carve out his own path of progress. Throughout his school life he had shown himself as receptive, indeed almost greedy of knowledge, painstaking and rather staid for his years. He took life, perhaps, too seriously, and was so much the model boy, that one almost longs to find some record of boyish pranks and delinquencies. Yet one gathers that he was not unpopular, either at school or at the university, where the same sobriety seems, on the whole, to have characterised him, and where he was commonly referred to as the "old man."

In some ways, however, this lack of understanding of schoolboy naughtiness handicapped him later, in his work as teacher, and put him somewhat out of sympathy with certain aspects of his pupils' lives. From Stuttgart he went in the year 1788 to the University of Tübingen. Destined for the Church, he held a bursary at the theological seminary in the town. Here he studied theology and philosophy, and pursued his own private reading. Finding the prescribed order of study rather arid and unfruitful, he devoted himself more and more to his own course of reading, which included not only classical but modern authors. Of the latter Rousseau, and later Kant, attracted him most. So absorbed did he become in his own studies that he often absented himself from lectures, and thereby incurred sundry penalties. He was clearly not so much the pattern university student as he had been the pattern schoolboy. His individual life was growing and expanding, and the cry of his heart was for freedom.

His friendship with Schelling dates from this period. They were both members of the political club which had been formed, and in which revolutionary views were discussed. Hegel remained at Tübingen for five years, and on leaving in 1793 decided to take a teaching post, not, it is to be feared, because he longed to teach, but mainly because he hoped to have more time and opportunity for self-development than in any other work.

The time of his best educational work was not yet. He must first make himself before he can throw himself heartily into the work of making others.

CHAPTER II

HEGEL'S TEACHING EXPERIENCE AS TUTOR AND LECTURER

As we have already noted, the name of Hegel is associated in the minds of most people only with the idea of a somewhat abstruse philosophy, strangely attractive or repellent, or perhaps merely incomprehensible, according to one's taste in such matters, so that it is rarely realised that he was for about fifteen years of his life a practical and an apparently successful teacher of youth.

For six years (1795 to 1801) he was a private tutor, first in Bern, and then in Frankfurt—while, later on, when about thirty-eight years of age, he was appointed Rector of the Gymnasium or Classical Secondary School for Boys at Nürnberg.

Of his work as private tutor we know but little. At Bern, where he held the post of tutor in the family of the Steigers von Tschugg, he had three pupils, two girls and a boy; the latter, Friedrich, being seven years of age when Hegel first took charge of him. There is reason to believe that another little boy—Perrot by name—was educated with the Steigers, but definite information is strangely lacking on all points connected with Hegel's teaching work in this post, and also in the similar one which he held for over three years in the Gogel family at Frankfurt am Main.

His silence with regard to this early teaching experience is in striking contrast to the detailed accounts we have of Herbart's work as a tutor. We feel as if we were personally acquainted with Herbart's pupils, we watch with him their gradual growth and development, and share his hopes and his fears for them. We can also trace the formation and unfolding of his educational views.

With Hegel, however, we have practically no clue. His pupils are not mentioned in his letters, nor do we find recorded any reflections upon education in general which might indicate the direction in which his thoughts on this subject were tending.

A partial explanation may be found in the fact that his first post at least was not altogether congenial—he could not make himself really at home in the Steiger family, and it is doubtful whether he was by nature at all suited to teach very young children. The somewhat grave and studious young man was probably unable to sympathise fully with these little Swiss children, who, living as they did, for a great part of the year, at their father's country house on the slopes of the Jura mountains, would no doubt have many interests which he, brought up in a town, would be unable to share. No doubt he did his best for them, but they were living in different worlds. He was at that stage in his development when the world of books and of thought was paramount, while to them the call of the sunshine, the lakes, woods and mountains was insistent : a call which was to him, at that time at least, incomprehensible. We gather from his diary kept during a walking tour in 1795,

made through some of the finest Alpine scenery, that it
did not much appeal to him.   The sight of the mountains
and the snow oppressed him, and only in the waterfalls,
which seemed to symbolise life, did he feel any real
delight.

He seems to have been far happier in his second post,
in the Gogel family.   It is probable that he understood
its members better, and he was also glad to be back once
more in Germany.   In Frankfurt too he found outside
interests, and made several valuable friendships.

In comparing him with Herbart, however, probably
the true explanation of the contrast between them is
to be found in their different types of mind and modes
of development.   With Herbart, action tends to come
first, reflection follows.   He is first a practical teacher,
and becomes a philosopher, mainly because of his interest
in education.   With Hegel the reverse is true, the
philosopher comes first and his practical work follows,
and is largely the outcome of his philosophy.   Hence
during these years in which his views of the universe
and of life were forming, we cannot expect to find him
doing his best practical work, although no doubt he
was almost unconsciously storing up experience which
would prove valuable later on.

One other point of difference between Herbart and
Hegel may perhaps be noted here.   Herbart tended to
view education from the psychological standpoint, and
much individual child observation and study almost
necessarily preceded any formulation of his ideas on
education.   Hegel, on the contrary, approached the
subject more from the metaphysical and sociological

sides. To Herbart, questions concerning the development of the individual mind—viz., formation of the circle of thought, many-sided interest, the good will, etc.—were of prime importance, while to Hegel the first points upon which he wished to be clear were the more general ones of the relation of education to the process of the world's evolution—to the State, to the family. This being the case, it was of course essential for Hegel to become in the first place sure of himself in regard to the problems of evolution, the State, and other fundamental conceptions, before considering or indeed being in a position to consider the real meaning and place of education.

His father died in 1799, leaving him a few hundred pounds, and this enabled him to give up his post as tutor and to go to Jena, where he spent the years 1801-1807. He delivered courses of lectures in the university, first as Privat-docent, and then as Professor Extraordinary (*i.e.* lecturing and receiving salary as a professor, but without holding an official position or taking part in university business).

It was at Jena also that he wrote the Phenomenology (*Phänomenologie des Geistes*), in which he gave a kind of first sketch of his philosophy. He called it his " Voyage of Discovery " ; in it indeed he has given us, as it were, a chart of all the region which later he was to make known to the world, with greater detail and exactness.

Unfortunately the war with France disturbed even the peace of university life, and after the battle of Jena Hegel found himself practically penniless, and with no prospect of future work at the university.

In these circumstances he was glad to undertake

B

a post as editor of a newspaper at Bamberg. This
arduous and not very congenial work he carried on in
a thoroughly businesslike way for about a year, until
more suitable work presented itself.

He had really obtained this post through the influence of his friend, Niethammer, who had held an
official position at Bamberg, but had just been appointed
director or head of the Protestant education department
for the kingdom of Bavaria. Hegel hoped that
Niethammer would find it possible to crown the
Bavarian educational system by the establishment of
a Protestant university, and with this in his mind he
wrote thus in his letter of congratulation, 23rd December
1807: "So best friend you will. certainly obtain or
prepare for us, a more or less Protestant University, and
then when thou comest into thy kingdom—remember
me." And Niethammer did remember him, and although
unable to fulfil his hopes of a post in a Bavarian university, secured for him the offer of the combined posts
of Professor of Philosophy and Rector of the Nürnberg
Gymnasium.

The year 1808 was an important and busy year for
Niethammer. In addition to all the practical work
involved in organising the Bavarian school system, he
found time to publish his book ("Streit des Philanthrop-
inismus und Humanismus in der Theorie des Erziehungs-
Unterrichts unser Zeit") dealing with the rival claims of
the classics and what might be called bread-and-butter
subjects, in which he maintains the importance and value
of the humanities as means of education, while recognising that other subjects have their place. At the time

when he was writing a fierce struggle was going on in regard to school curricula. On the one hand the advocates of the older education urged the disciplinary value of the classics and especially of Latin Grammar, while the more revolutionary educationists insisted on the importance of subjects which bore more directly upon everyday life and had technical as well as training value. Niethammer was in favour of a middle course, in which both sides of education should be provided for. He advocated reform in the teaching of the classics, but urged that the really human side of man, his intellect and spirit, needed to be nourished, and could only be properly nourished through the study of the humanities, to which also he added Philosophy and Religion. Scientific and more technical studies were not to be neglected, however, and were to find due place even in the gymnasium or classical school.

He worked out a new plan or scheme of schools and studies (Schulplan) för Bavaria, which came into force in November 1808 and was announced to the School Authorities as : The general Normativ (scheme or code) for the regulation of public educational institutions. Provision was made in the Normativ for schools of all types, including the elementary schools (Volksschule) ; preparatory schools (Primar Schule and Progymnasium) ; real or middle-class schools, science or technical schools (Real Instituten), and classical schools (Gymnasien).

The Normativ is an interesting document, in which Niethammer sets forth not only regulations for the organisation and management of these various types of school, but also their curricula. He gives with con-

siderable detail the subjects to be taught, their scope
and order, and discourses with zest on their several
educational values.   There is a fine air of leisureliness
and also of enthusiasm about it, which makes it
pleasant reading.   One feels that it was drawn up
by no mere official, but by one who really cared for
education.   It is not surprising, therefore, to find that
he and Hegel genuinely admired each other and were
anxious to work together in the cause of education,
and many letters passed between them, dealing almost
entirely with educational questions.

The Normativ was not yet published, however, when
Niethammer wrote to Hegel (October 1808) in the
following terms :—

"I have to inform you that you have been nominated
as Professor of Philosophy and Rector of the Nürnberg
Gymnasium."

Niethammer regarded it as very important that these
two posts should be combined, and intended this to be the
case in all the Bavarian gymnasien.   It was, however,
only at Nürnberg that his wish was fulfilled.   No doubt
his real reason was that he desired that religious, moral,
and philosophical instruction should be in the hands of
one person, and that one the headmaster.

Hegel did not take long to make up his mind.   In
connection with his philosophy he had begun to reflect
upon educational problems and was becoming fully
alive to their importance.   We find him stating in the
"Phänomenologie" that it is only through education and
culture that the individual attains real value, and even
real existence as an individual, and also further urging the

importance of language as a means of education. Feeling himself to be largely in sympathy with Niethammer's general views on education, and especially with his desire both to reform and to secure instruction in the classics ; glad also to have the chance of teaching philosophy and of trying the experiment of adapting the subject to school-boy powers of comprehension, Hegel had no hesitation in accepting the position now offered him.

CHAPTER III

RECTOR OF NÜRNBERG GYMNASIUM

HEGEL entered upon his new duties in December 1808.

Nürnberg was well provided with schools of every type, so that there was no difficulty in making the gymnasium from the first what it was intended to be— a classical secondary school for boys. For those whose parents desired another kind of education there was ample provision in the town. The difficulties that Hegel had to contend against were of another kind.

The building was an old school, rather hastily adapted to meet the needs of the new institution, and the result was far from satisfactory. The surroundings were squalid, the accommodation inadequate and unhygienic ; school furniture and apparatus defective ; suitable supplies of stationery and books were not at first forthcoming, and indeed the school must have appeared to Hegel on first acquaintance as most dreary and unpromising. It speaks well for his practical gifts, his energy and organising power, that, in spite of all these very real difficulties, the school was a success from the first. Indeed he proved himself to be in every way a most competent headmaster, and was successful both as organiser and as teacher. He was strong just where Pestalozzi and many another great teacher has proved himself weak—in business capacity and power of government. It was not for nothing that he came of a race of competent civil servants, accustomed to undertake responsibility and to perform careful, detailed and methodical work. He had no doubt been brought up to consider that all work done for the State was worthy of a man's best effort, and in his writings we find repeated evidence that he regarded education as a State function, and teachers as civil servants. We can well believe that no detail of the school arrangements was beneath his notice and that, keeping his hand constantly and firmly on the reins, he would guide all the varied elements of school work to a successful issue.

The organisation of the school was somewhat complicated. The gymnasium proper had a four - year course and was intended for boys between the ages of fourteen and eighteen. It had three classes—upper, middle and lower—but boys were expected to spend two years in the middle class, which had two divisions. Pupils from twelve to fourteen were provided for in the progymnasium, which had two classes. Below these again came the Primary school (Primar, not Volksschule) with two divisions, the upper and the lower, in each of which (at least after the first year) there were two classes. Boys might be admitted to the lower primary school at the age of eight. For some years there was a still lower division of the school, consisting of the two " Collaboratur-Klassen," to which were admitted younger boys, and especially those who were backward or not sufficiently prepared to be able to profit by the regular work of the school. On the advice of Hegel these classes were soon discontinued, and those seeking ad-

mission to the school were required to show their fitness
by passing before entrance a simple examination, of
which, however, the elements of Latin formed a compulsory part.

The following table shows the organisation of the school
in the first, second and seventh years of Hegel's rector-
ship, and gives the number of pupils in each class :—

THE ROYAL GYMNASIAL INSTITUTION AT NÜRNBERG

1808-9.
    I. GYMNASIUM—

(a) Upper Class .	.	. Number of pupils—12	⎫
(b) Middle Class	.	. ,, ,, —13	⎬ 36
(c) Lower Class .	.	. ,, ,, —11	⎭

    II. PROGYMNASIUM—

(a) Upper Class .	.	. ,, ,, — 6	⎫ 18
(b) Lower Class .	.	. ,, ,, —12	⎭

    III. PRIMARY OR PREPARATORY SCHOOLS—

(a) Upper Primary School	. ,,	,, —27	⎫ 58
(b) Lower Primary School	. ,,	,, —31	⎭

    IV. AUXILIARY CLASSES (Collaboratur-Klassen)—

(a)	,, ,, —33	⎫ 63
(b)	,, ,, —30	⎭

                 Total number of pupils in school .   .   175

1809-10.
    I. GYMNASIUM—

(a) Upper Class .	.	. Number of pupils— 9	⎫
(b) Middle Class, 2nd course or year	,,	,, — 4	⎬ 29
Middle Class, 1st course	. ,,	,, — 7	⎪
(c) Lower Class .	.	. ,, ,, — 9	⎭

    II. PROGYMNASIUM—

(a) Upper Class .	.	. ,, ,, —14	⎫ 31
(b) Lower Class .	.	. ,, ,, —17	⎭

III. PRIMARY SCHOOLS—
    (*a*) Upper Primary, 2nd course
      or year .   .   . Number of pupils— 7 ⎫
    Upper Primary, 1st course .   ,,   ,, —17 ⎪
    (*b*) Lower Primary, 2nd course .   ,,   ,, — 7 ⎬ 55
    Lower Primary, 1st course .   ,,   ,, —24 ⎭

IV. AUXILIARY CLASSES—
    (*a*)   ,,   ,, —35 ⎫
    (*b*)   ,,   ,, —43 ⎬ 78
         Total number of pupils in school .   . 193

1814-15.
I. GYMNASIUM—
    (*a*) Upper Class.   .   . Number of pupils—12 ⎫
    (*b*) Middle Class, 2nd course or
      year   .   .   .   ,,   ,, — 9 ⎬ 48
      Middle Class, 1st course .   ,,   ,, —10 ⎪
    (*c*) Lower Class.   .   .   ,,   ,, —17 ⎭

II. PROGYMNASIUM—
    (*a*) Upper Class .   .   .   ,   ,, —16 ⎫
    (*b*) Lower Class .   .   .   ,,   ,, —18 ⎬ 34

III. PRIMARY SCHOOLS—
    (*a*) Upper Primary, 2nd course
      or year .   .   .   ,,   ,, —24 ⎫
    Upper Primary, 1st course .   ,,   ,, —32 ⎪
    (*b*) Lower Primary, 2nd course.   ,,   ,, —25 ⎬ 99
    Lower Primary, 1st course .   ,,   ,, —18 ⎭
        Total number of pupils in school .   . 181

It should be noted that the apparent decrease in numbers is due to the giving up of the auxiliary classes; leaving those out of account, it will be seen that there had been a steady increase in the number of pupils attending the regular school classes.

The subjects of the curriculum and the amount of time to be devoted to each were for the most part clearly set forth in the Normativ. A translation of that portion which deals with the above is given further on.

According to Niethammer's code, *Latin and Greek* come first in order of importance, and claim more time than any other subject.

In the primary schools, Latin only is studied, and the boys are required to devote at least 10 hours weekly to the subject. In the progymnasium, where Greek is begun with 7 hours per week, Latin drops to 6 hours and in the higher classes from 10 to 12 hours are divided between the two languages and their literatures.

French is given 3 hours per week, beginning in the upper primary school.

German, as the mother tongue, is studied in the lower classes at least. It seems likely that about 6 hours weekly would be available for this purpose in the primary schools.

History, treated as General History, is allotted 4 hours weekly in the upper primary school and progymnasium —as a study of Special Historical Periods it has 4 hours in the upper middle class of the gymnasium and the same amount in the highest gymnasial class.

Geography is to be taught for 4 hours per week in the lower primary school; and for 3 hours in the progymnasium and 2 hours in the lowest gymnasium class.

Mathematics (Arithmetic, Algebra and Geometry) claims 3 hours weekly in the primary schools and progymnasium and 4 hours in the classes of the gymnasium.

Writing is given 6 hours in the lower and 3 hours in the upper primary schools, combined with *Drawing*. 6 hours weekly are arranged for in the progymnasium.

Physiography and *Cosmography* get some attention in the gymnasium, and as the school grew and developed Hegel introduced a certain amount of more regular study of *Science*.

To *Religious and Moral Instruction* 3 hours weekly are given in the primary schools and 2 hours in the pro-gymnasium. In the gymnasium these, combined with an introductory course in Philosophy (including Logic and Psychology), are allotted 4 hours per week.

The total weekly number of teaching hours in the primary schools and progymnasium was to be 32, while in the gymnasium itself a total of 27 was deemed suffi-cient, no doubt in view of the fact that the older boys would give more time to home preparation.

Hegel's own account of the school curriculum, as he gives it at the end of his first year as headmaster, differs but slightly from what is laid down in the Normativ.

" The study of the ancients in their own languages and the study of grammar form the fundamental features of instruction which distinguish our institution. This great possession, valuable as it is in itself, does not however exhaust the whole compass of the subjects taught in our school.

" The course of reading in the classics is so chosen as to include a rich content of instruction, and in addition the school undertakes to teach other subjects which have a value in themselves or are of special utility or attractiveness.

" These need only be named here ; the special courses in these subjects, their scope, methods and relations with other subjects, also the various exercises connected with them, are to be seen in more detail in the printed prospectus.

" Broadly speaking, these subjects are the following :— Religious instruction, the German language including an acquaintance with its standard literature, Arithmetic (later on Algebra), Geometry, Geography, History, Physiography — which includes Cosmography, Natural History and Natural Philosophy, subjects which prepare for Philosophy (philosophische Vorbereitungswissenshaften) ; French ; for the future theologian Hebrew ; Drawing and writing.

" How little these subjects are neglected is shown by the simple calculation, that if we do not take into account the four last subjects, the teaching hours are seen to be divided equally between the classics and the above-mentioned subjects and if we take into account the four subjects left out, we find that the study of the classics occupies not half but only two-fifths of the whole time devoted to instruction."

It will be noticed that the chief points in which Hegel's account of the course of study differs from the Normativ is in the inclusion of Natural History, and some Science (Natural Philosophy) ; the greater emphasis laid upon the study of the national language and literature and the introduction of the study of Hebrew.

But Hegel not only drew up his time-table with care and organised the instruction given in school—he also made careful arrangements for home work and used his best efforts to secure the co-operation of the parents in carrying these out.

" In order that the instruction given in the school

shall be fruitful, that the pupils shall make real progress, *private study* and diligence on their part are as
necessary as teaching itself."

" Special value attaches to the pupil's own work
and to what he does at home in connection with the
instruction given at school. For this home work the
co-operation of the parents with us is essential ; inasmuch as pride in maintaining a good position amongst
their comrades, desire to win the approval of teachers
and gain the sense of self-satisfaction resulting from duty
fulfilled, have not yet attained the necessary strength
to be effective. This is especially the case in the early
years of school life when the habit of independent work
has not yet been formed, and also in later years when the
desire for diversion and social life begins to disturb the
minds of the young." [1]

Hegel impressed upon his assistant masters the importance of regularity in giving out and correcting home
work. He insisted on the exercises being carefully
prepared and given in to time.

" Boys must not be allowed to neglect their work
or to send it in late. Nothing is worse than to allow
them to get into careless ways in this respect." [2]

He held that boys must learn to work by themselves,
and that their home work should therefore not consist
merely in reproduction, but should also involve some
independent thought and work.

In another matter also Hegel secured the co-operation
of his assistants. Careful written reports were made
on each pupil by the masters who taught him, and these

[1] Vol. viii. 133.   [2] XVI. Second address.

were read out in each class so that the work and conduct of each boy was judged in the presence of his classmates. The boys took places in their forms according to these reports, and all advance from form to form in the school depended on them.

Parents could have copies of these reports if they desired them. At the prize-giving functions the final class lists for the year were read publicly, and afterwards printed.

Hegel was, however, careful to explain both to the boys and to the parents that quick promotion up the school was not always possible or desirable. Boys are not all alike. Some develop much more quickly than others and it would be a great mistake to promote a boy who was not ready; in the end, indeed, it would really retard his progress.

CHAPTER IV

HEGEL AS TEACHER AND DISCIPLINARIAN

FOR the first school year Hegel seems to have acted as form master to the highest class in the gymnasium, and to have taught the boys in that form mathematics.

We find in his report on the work of that year that "the class made fair progress in Algebra (Proportion, Progressions and Logarithms, also equations of the second degree), but that in Geometry only three books of Euclid had been worked through.'[1] After the first year Hegel does not appear to have had a form of his own, and indeed his hands were full enough without it.

He took entire charge of the philosophical, moral and religious teachings in the gymnasium, giving four hours a week to each of the three classes (presumably the two middle divisions were taken together), thus devoting at least twelve hours per week to teaching. It is also probable that he took some share in the religious instruction given lower down in the school; it has indeed been suggested that he took the whole of it, but with all his

---

[1] The note of dissatisfaction is probably due to the fact that the boys, owing to lack of previous training, needed to be taught the elements of Geometry.

other duties it is hardly likely that this was the case. He was unusually well equipped for the post of head-master, by reason of his wide knowledge and interests. No subject came amiss to him, and we are told that the boys were greatly impressed by the ease and readiness with which he took over the work of any master who was absent through illness or other cause. Whatever the subject of the lesson—Latin, Greek, Mathematics, History, French or Cosmology—he was ready almost at a moment's notice to unfold his stores of knowledge, and in such a way as to interest and rouse mental activity.

In spite of his lack of power as an orator, he appears to have been a really good teacher, and this no doubt largely because of the trouble he took (whenever possible) in preparing the lessons he gave and the attention he paid to method and arrangement, but above all his success was probably due to the fact that he really cared for, and was for the time absorbed in what he was teaching. Genuine enthusiasm for knowledge is in-fectious, and the boys were doubtless directly influenced by his personal attitude towards learning and often carried away by his earnestness and the real interest he displayed in the subject before them.

As far as possible he adopted the conversational method, asking many questions himself and especially trying to encourage the boys to ask questions themselves, or to raise points for discussion. Yet at the same time his teaching was never desultory, he kept his classes well in hand, and questions and discussions always led to some definite point. He often began his teaching by dictating a short paragraph, and then spent the rest of the time in elucidating and amplifying this concise statement of the matter of the lesson. The boys took notes of the points raised, and discussed and were expected to reproduce the substance of the whole lesson afterwards—either orally or in writing. If the exercises were written they were carefully looked over, and corrected by Hegel himself.

Sometimes he would begin the hour by calling upon one or more of the pupils to summarise orally what had been dealt with in the last lesson, or the material thus gained was often required to be used as the substance of a written Latin exercise.

His chief aim was to secure that the boys really understood and could make use of what they learned.   He was glad even to be interrupted in what he was saying if a pupil did not understand, but laziness and inattention he could not tolerate.

He was always anxious to develop in the boys a taste for good reading, and they were encouraged to come to him privately, in order to consult him as to what books they should choose.   They were almost always advised to read old books rather than new, those that had stood the test of time rather than those still in process of being judged.

After some difficulty he managed to start a school library, in the growth of which he took great pride and care and encouraged the boys to do the same.

Whenever a new book or books of interest were added to the library it was his custom to assemble the boys in the gymnasial classes and give them collectively some

C

account of the works in question, thus securing many an opportunity for cultivating in them a love of good literature.

Nor were more scientific interests neglected. Before he left the school Hegel had made an excellent beginning of what might be called a school museum.

In his yearly public school addresses from time to time he made grateful references to presents made to the school—of books, old coins, specimens of minerals and the like—and no doubt his practice had the effect of making the wants of the school known and of stimulating generosity in this direction.

Hegel gained the reputation of being a stern disciplinarian, and it is true that he had small sympathy with rowdiness, practical jokes or disorder of any kind, and never failed to deal with such firmly and even severely. Perhaps he tended to judge too seriously what might often have been mere exuberance of boyish spirits, but on the whole his sternness towards all wrongdoing had no ill effects and was probably necessary and salutary in those exciting years when revolt and revolution were still so much in the air.

He put down smoking, and discouraged fighting and amateur duelling amongst the boys. On the other hand he introduced military drill and exercises into the school, and felt so strongly on the subject of their value and importance that he devoted a portion of one of his school addresses to urging the claims of this kind of training to serious consideration and attention on the part of both parents and boys. He was, we fear, not quite sound on the matter of school games ; they were allowed, but the school did practically nothing to promote them. When we consider, however, that even at the present day school games are not regarded in Germany as being so important a part of social and moral education as is the case in England, we shall not perhaps be surprised at his failure to realise their use and value.

Indeed on the whole, and especially when we remember that he had no natural taste for games and ordinary amusements, he was really very tolerant in the matter. We learn that he would sometimes watch the boys playing, and thus indirectly encourage them, and he even permitted those boys who desired to do so to learn dancing in the school.

In connection with this latter, an amusing story is told, which throws an interesting light on his methods of dealing with the boys. In the year 1812 a good many of the pupils desired to form a dancing class, and Hegel allowed them to do so, although no doubt he had little sympathy with their taste.

The dancing master, however, proved disappointing. The boys thought him conceited and foppish, and grew impatient of being restricted by him to the practice of steps and bows, when they had hoped for more exciting entertainment. Finally they determined to appeal to their rector for permission to withdraw from the classes, and a small deputation was appointed to wait upon him. The two boys chosen went up to his room with hope and confidence in their cause, but, as one of them (Lochner) has placed on record — they never knew how they got out of the room and down the stairs again.

Hegel was not one to tolerate fickleness and unsettled purpose. What had been begun must be finished ; each must abide the consequences of his own actions. As they had undertaken to dance, dance they must until the school year was over. Besides, the dancing master had been led to expect a certain amount in fees and must not be defrauded.

Surprised and overawed, the boys retreated precipitately, and no further word was heard about withdrawal from the dancing classes.

His general relations with both staff and pupils seem to have been most cordial in character. He showed himself friendly to all, and took personal interest in each one. When boys were about to leave school he made a point of seeing them individually, and of talking to them about their future pursuits. If they were proceeding to the university he would discuss with them the questions of their academic career and final choice of a profession, and also give them hints as to methods of independent study.

This was in addition to the public word of admonition and encouragement which he usually had for them at some point in his annual address. The following lines, taken from his 1809 address, afford a good illustration of his method of exhortation :

" In our fatherland every career is open to your talents and application, but only by merit is advance possible. Bravely continue at the university the work you have begun here. Most of you leave your homes for the first time ; you . . . part from the family life in order to take the necessary step towards independence. Youth looks forward ; in doing so, however, never forget the backward look of gratitude, of love and duty towards your parents."

Some of his old boys have testified to the reverence and admiration with which he was regarded by his pupils. They were proud of having a man of his reputation as their headmaster. The sterling worth of his character, his simple life and stern devotion to duty, made a deep, if partly unconscious, impression upon them. They would hear him spoken of in the town as a man of philosophical and literary attainments, and no doubt they were quite aware (for not much escapes the curiosity of boys in respect of their teachers) that he was engaged in writing important books. Then too they would note how even his recreation consisted largely in reading newspapers belonging to other countries. He would often be seen by them in the evening poring over these papers in the town library, and his reputation as an authority on world politics would be established.

Keenly interested as he was in politics, and well abreast of all the political questions of the day, he yet thought it his duty as Rector of the Gymnasium to abstain not only from all active participation in political work, but even from definite expressions of opinion. At heart a keen patriot, and longing to see his country rise to a sense of her true national life, he yet with wonderful self-restraint refrained from taking any part in the movement. He held that schoolboys should have no present-day political opinions : the past and not the present—the far-off and foreign to their nature, and not that which is immediate in its effects, give the necessary conditions for educational development.

Likewise he feared the effect of any emotional strain on these immature minds. Even in maintaining ordinary school discipline, he was careful to appeal rather to reason than to the feelings. At secondary school age duty should be done because it is seen to be duty, not on account of affection or of fear.

Holding these strong convictions, he believed that his position as headmaster required not only that he should take no share in politics himself, but also that he should not countenance anything of the kind in connection with his school.

But the wave of national political feeling ran high in Nürnberg, and it needed all Hegel's tact and discretion to deal with its influence on his pupils.

The following gives an instance of the wise and somewhat humorous way in which he went to work.

Many of the boys had banded themselves together in a society to which they gave the name of " The German Union." They used to meet to discuss papers written by members bearing on the problems of German nationalism, and much enthusiasm and interest was roused in the school. Hegel, on hearing of it, sent for the leaders and praised their industry and desire for political knowledge and their wish to be helpful to their country. But he suggested that, as a firm grasp of political principles necessarily involved clear views as to the growth and development of the idea of the " State," they should first devote their attention to the building up of that idea in classical times. He proposed therefore that the society should now, under his guidance, turn its attention in the first place to a serious study of Homer. It is to be feared that the proposition was not hailed with the enthusiasm it deserved. No one could accuse Hegel of persecuting the society or those belonging to it, but somehow it disappeared as a school organisation, and those boys who still wished to discuss the national politics of the time held their meetings outside the school buildings.

Of course his attitude of aloofness led to much misapprehension and misrepresentation.

He was even sometimes called a " Frenchman," to draw attention to his supposed anti-patriotic leanings. This outside criticism, however, he could afford to disregard, and there is no evidence to show that he was ever so misjudged inside his school.

In time indeed he came to hold a very strong and influential position in Nürnberg. He had friendly relations with the other teachers of the town and the professors of the neighbouring university at Erlangen. His election as member (Schulrath) of the Schools Council in 1813 indicates that he was already regarded as an authority on matters connected with education.

His annual school addresses, delivered to the pupils, their parents and friends, were useful in bringing the school and its work before the public eye, and Hegel was accustomed on these occasions to take everyone discreetly into his confidence with regard to the aims and objects, the curriculum, methods and discipline of the school. Changes on the staff, new arrangements with regard to classes, reports, etc., all are

treated of with a simple directness that must have
disarmed criticism.

These addresses are really wonderful examples of the
possibility of combining the theoretical and the practical,
the philosophic view of education brought into relation
with the necessary details of school organisation and
method.

In many striking and beautiful passages he sets forth
his philosophy in educational form. It is doubtful
whether his hearers would always have been able to follow
him, for Hegel was very thorough-going in applying
even his most abstruse philosophical views to education,
but fortunately his audience was never kept too long
on the stretch, and after his most eloquent flights he was
accustomed to return quickly and easily to matters of
more practical interest.

The addresses were delivered on the occasions of the
annual prize-giving, which served at the same time as a
sort of farewell function (somewhat corresponding to the
High School " Commencement " in the United States)
for those leaving for the university.

The prizes were given by the State, and it was so much
Hegel's custom to uphold everything done by the State
that it is difficult to know whether he really approved
of the principle of tangible rewards in connection with
education. It is probable, however, that in any case
he had no strong feeling against them. We know that
he regarded punishment as the right of the wrongdoer,
absolutely necessary for his proper evolution, and it
may be that he looked upon rewards and prizes as
being also earned and therefore not justly to be with-

held. On one occasion (September 1810), before proceeding to the prize distribution, he tries to impress
upon those who are about to be recipients a sense of
the proper spirit in which the prizes should be taken.
" Receive one," he says, " as a token of satisfaction with
that which you have already accomplished, and still more
as a new demand on your further efforts—as a higher
claim upon you from your parents, your teachers and
your fatherland ! "

Only five of these addresses have been preserved :
those of his first, second, third, fifth and seventh years of
office. The first of these, which was delivered on 29th
September 1809, deals with the organisation of the school
as a classical gymnasium. In it he makes a fine defence
of classical studies and urges the importance of the study
both of language and of literature.

In the second, given on 14th September 1810, he unfolds the idea of discipline : proper government and the
relation of regulated class and private work in their
effects on the order and general tone of the school ; the
introduction of military drill and the value and importance of these systematic physical exercises. The
address concludes with a consideration of the relation
of moral training and instruction to intellectual
education.

On 2nd September 1811 the subject mainly dealt with
was the school regarded as medium between family and
public life.

In his address delivered on 2nd September 1813 he
again urges the importance of classical studies. In the
classics the *unity* of man's life is always emphasised, and

therefore these serve as an antidote to the present-day tendency towards over-specialisation in some particular calling or profession.

In that of the 30th August 1814, the last of which we have any record, he points out the sad effect upon the young at the present day of the strife between New and Old. The result is that they are in a state of ferment and unrest and, having no sure foundations in themselves, too easily become prey to an empty formalism.

Hegel blames the too early participation of children in the distractions and pleasures of grown-up people, and urges that they require quiet and undisturbed opportunities for growth.

He was always anxious to secure the active co-operation of the parents with the school in the work of education, and did not shrink from very plain speaking when occasion seemed to demand it.

We find him trying to impress upon the parents that the influence and responsibility of a day school were necessarily limited and that the school must not be expected to assume the duties of the home.   But while he was anxious that the parents should do their share he, on his part, always endeavoured to support home influence.   A striking instance of this is to be found in his attitude towards religious observance.   He did his best to secure that his pupils should not only attend public worship with their parents on Sundays, but even arranged for them to keep the religious festivals of their respective Churches, and although naturally with Protestant sympathies himself, the Roman Catholics attending his school were kept to their religious duties as strictly as the others. It would be interesting to know what happened with regard to religious instruction in the school, whether the Catholic boys were excused or had to attend only the moral and philosophical instruction classes, but on this point unfortunately we have no light. In any case the majority of the boys would have been Protestants.

In considering the period of Hegel's teaching activity at Nürnberg it is specially striking to note the way in which he not only made the best of the existing conditions of education but even seemed to be content with them. It was as if he felt able to interpret the actual in terms of the ideal. Indeed for him the ideal was never merely the far-off, unattained and dim, it was rather to be sought for here and now, in the work that lies nearest to hand. In the living present is to be found all that is necessary for growth, and only by right use of existing institutions is any true progress to be realised. The Family, the School and the State, as they exist in any given age, mark out the road along which evolution must take place. There must be advance and improvement indeed, but these are to be secured through and not in opposition to these institutions. It was just here that he was out of sympathy with those who, like Rousseau and Basedow, would pull down, and completely alter existing conditions, and even with Kant, who urged that we should educate the young for the conceivably much improved future. These in the name of reason and humanity call upon us to break away from the past and present in order to secure real progress. To Hegel, on the contrary, the actual is the rational, what we have the only sure foundation for what is to be.

The following passage from his fourth address seems to bear on this point : " The proverb ' the better is the enemy of the good ' is full of meaning ; it impresses on us that striving after the better, if it becomes a passion, does not allow the good to develop and mature.   If law and order—which should constitute the firm foundation and support for any future necessary changes, should themselves become insecure, whereon shall that which is in its very nature variable establish itself ? Institutions are indeed affected by progress, but this advance is slow ; a single year is here unmeaning ; changes in them mark great and rare epochs."

CHAPTER V

MARRIAGE AND LATER LIFE

ENGROSSED as he was with the work of the school, there were two other interests in his life at this period, which we must now consider briefly.

In April 1811 he became engaged to Marie von Tucher, a charming girl of twenty, belonging to an old distinguished Nürnberg family. She was the eldest of seven children, and as her parents were far from well off no obstacle was put in the way of an early marriage— which took place in September of that year.

In spite of the inequality of age and of certain differences in temperament and tastes, the marriage proved very happy. She is said to have had pleasant, graceful manners, to have been very quick, impulsive and affectionate—not by any means the German Hausfrau of tradition. They made a real pair of opposites—she with her youthful, delicate, aristocratic air; he with his middle-aged gravity and solidity, his somewhat bourgeois appearance and Swabian accent.

Yet one gathers that he was not unattractive even in looks and that, at this period of his life at least, he was very careful about his dress. As he grew older he may have become absent-minded and careless in the matter —such stories as that of his leaving one of his shoes behind him in the mud on his way to lecture at the University of Heidelberg, or of his wearing a yellow-grey dressing-gown when interviewing a student, tend to linger in the memory—but in his Nürnberg days we learn that he was always suitably, if quietly, dressed in a grey suit and immaculate linen.

In mind and temperament he and his wife were clearly very different. Hers was the quick, intuitive mind which takes small account of logical process, and yet reaches conclusions—often and perhaps generally correct ; while his, in spite of his mystical tendencies, was rather of the hard, intellectual type that arrives at its conclusions, or at least those which are trusted, only after careful thought, in which every step of logical reasoning is made clear. From their letters it would seem that sometimes they failed to understand each other on this account, and no doubt each would occasionally find the other rather trying, But fortunately they had a common meeting ground in their love for the fine arts—music, painting and sculpture as well as poetry attracted them both—and as after all Hegel was one of those who work alone, who in philosophy must plough a lonely furrow, it was perhaps just as well that the tastes they had in common were those which occupied for them the leisure rather than the strenuous side of life.

There is no doubt that on the whole the marriage was an unusually happy one. They were never rich, and always had to live carefully, keeping only one servant and practising many little economies, but Hegel seems to have lightened the burden of house-

keeping and management for his wife by wise fore-
thought. Again, his practical gifts and capacity for
detail stood him in good stead. We hear of his
arranging some little surprise or planning some simple
excursion for his wife and family, and when he was
away from home, writing long letters to his wife, telling
of all that he had seen of interest.

They had two sons, Karl, named after his grandfather
on the mother's side, and Immanuel, named after Hegel's
friend, Niethammer.[1] Another absorbing interest of
the Nürnberg period was his great book—the *Logic*.
At this he was working during most of the years of his
school work and it was published just as he was leaving
in 1816.

As time went on, and his philosophy grew and developed
in his mind, he began to long for the greater freedom of
university life and the opportunity of teaching philosophy to more mature minds.

In July 1816 he was suddenly offered three chairs
of Philosophy at once—viz., those of Berlin, Heidelberg
and Erlangen.

For reasons which need not be entered into here, he
chose Heidelberg, where he took up his duties in the
autumn.

After two years of work at the university, during
which time he wrote the *Encyclopædie*, he made
his final move to Berlin in 1818. Here, surrounded by
eager students and disciples, and with a growing reputation and influence, he pursued his philosophical work
until his death from cholera in 1831.

[1] Karl afterwards became Professor of History at Erlangen.

With his work at Heidelberg and at Berlin we are not
here directly concerned, but it is interesting to note
that although he left his work as a schoolmaster behind
him its valuable effects were not lost. In the first
place, there is no doubt that he taught philosophy
better in the university because he had taught it in the
school. He himself acknowledges that the necessary
attempt to simplify philosophical ideas, in order to bring
them within the comprehension of immature minds, was
of the utmost value in clarifying his own views and in
enabling him to make the foundations of his philosophy
firm and sure.

The necessity for this firm foundation became so
apparent to him that in the university he always
endeavoured to be a real *teacher* of philosophy and not
merely one who studied and professed the subject.
He tells us: "I am a schoolmaster who has to teach
philosophy, and perhaps partly for that reason, am
possessed with the idea that philosophy, as truly as
geometry, must be a regular structure of ideas which is
capable of being taught."

Then, too, there is no reason to suppose that he lost
his interest in school education when he ceased to be a
schoolmaster. Although ceasing to work directly in
this way, it seems clear that he continued to exercise a
most important indirect influence over education.

We know that Rosenkranz, a Berlin student and Hegel's
enthusiastic biographer, devoted much of his time and
energy to educational work when Professor of Philosophy at Königsberg ; that he not only lectured on
education, but trained teachers and conducted a demon-

stration school. It would seem to be more than probable that he was inspired to do so by Hegel himself, and that he believed that he was in this educational work giving effect to an important aspect of his master's teaching.

It has already been pointed out that he exercised a very important influence over Prussian education, largely, no doubt, because some of his philosophical followers held office there.

So much indeed was this the case that a recent writer has said: "His philosophy may well be called the Prussian state philosophy during the years from 1820 to 1840. It was the philosophical system officially acknowledged by the Ministry of Education." [1]

His educational work too in Bavaria was not forgotten. He had set a high standard of work and efficiency for schools of the gymnasial type, and the gymnasium at Nürnberg remains to this day as a monument of Hegel's splendid initial work during the years of his headmastership.

[1] Paulsen, "German Universities."

PART II

HEGEL'S CHIEF CONTRIBUTIONS TO THEORY OF EDUCATION AND PEDAGOGY

CHAPTER VI

GENERAL POSITION IN REGARD TO EDUCATIONAL THEORY

In attempting to estimate the significance of the educational views put forward by any writer, it is of the first importance that his general philosophical position should be taken into account. The place and value assigned to education must vary considerably, according to the view taken of life—its meaning, permanence and worth. In the case of Hegel it is particularly necessary to do so, as much of his pedagogy would be almost unintelligible unless studied in the light of his philosophic theory.

But of course it may be urged that Hegel did not give and never contemplated giving to the world a Theory of Education or System of Pedagogy ; that his connection with education was purely practical, and that he regarded the work of a teacher (including his own) as ranking as that of a civil servant, called upon to forward in this way a necessary part of the business of the State. Even if we admit partially the truth of this latter statement, however, we must remember that the service of the State meant to him far more than earning a livelihood. The State was for him the embodied life of the people, in whose cause it was well to spend and be spent and whose service demanded the best he had to give in the way of intellectual, moral and physical effort.

What perhaps does at first sight seem to lend colour to the view that Hegel had no educational theory is the fact that he has left us no systematic treatise, and nowhere in his writings does he even attempt to sum up his general views on the subject It was so much the custom in his day for philosophers to write and lecture on education that this omission on his part is all the more marked. It is only by careful study of his general philosophical writings, his letters and the addresses which he delivered as Rector of the Nürnberg Gymnasium, that we are able to discover and to piece together, as it were, the theory that underlay his practice.

Yet this in itself is not without significance, and suggests that perhaps the omission was not unintentional—that he really viewed education as so much a necessary part of the life process that it could only be understood and adequately treated in connection with the philosophy of life as a whole. On reflection it will be seen that ethics is in much the same case. Hegel has left no separate treatise on ethics [1] and it might be similarly (although few would do so seriously) urged that therefore he regarded morality and the ethical life in general as belonging entirely to the realm of practice and not as a subject for philosophic consideration.

At this point too it may be well to consider what we

[1] Unless we class his Philosophy of Right as such, but it obviously covers a much wider field and indeed includes some consideration of the subject of education.

really mean when we refer to a person's Theory of
Education. It is a term that we are apt to use somewhat glibly, and without always realising the breadth of
its connotation. Strictly speaking, it might be said
that no one has yet produced, nor is it likely that anyone
will produce, a Theory of Education complete in all its
branches.

The concept of education is so wide, so comprehensive,
that it seems doubtful whether one human being could
unite in himself all the qualities and experience necessary
for the adequate performance of the task. Education
needs to be considered in so many relations—*e.g.* to a
general philosophy of life; to special sciences (particularly
to psychology and physiology); to sociological and
economic conditions; to legislation and the State; to
practice (with its many problems of method, organisation, equipment), etc.—and it is obvious that no one
person is likely to do equal justice to all these several
aspects of the subject.

Those who have done most to promote the cause of
education have usually confined themselves to one or
two of these, or at least it may be said that their really
permanent contributions have been so limited. Consider, by way of illustration, the respective contributions
to educational theory made by Locke, Herbart and
Froebel. It is obvious that they all had something
of value to say on the subject, but the emphasis in
each case is different. We turn to Locke for his wise,
common-sense views of the sound mind in the sound
body. Even when he seems to become somewhat extreme, as in the matter of hardening and habit, or when

his psychology and ethics fail to satisfy us, we yet feel that he was a pioneer in his attempt to apply the laws of physiology and hygiene, psychology, logic and ethics to the solution of the problem of education, and do not blame him for not treating also of school organisation, legislation or the metaphysical aspects of education. Herbart has given us what is probably the most complete theory of method ever formulated. We may differ from his views as to the ultimate constitution of mind and its mode of growth and development, but the practical value of his analysis of the teaching process, the emphasis he lays upon the importance of character-building and its connection with instruction, make his contributions to educational theory one of the most valuable of modern times, and yet there are obviously whole areas left practically untouched.

Froebel, again, although we know he had a definite philosophy of life, and much interest in sociological aspects of education, has yet made his really lasting contribution in connection with the training of little children at the stage when, as he puts it, "the inner must be made outer," when manifold expression is the real need. This is the stage before that of ordinary school instruction—when the outer has to be made inner— the age of formal instruction, in respect of which Herbart's reputation is deservedly greater.

Similarly Hegel's contribution to educational theory is limited, and moreover in the main to such problems as make no obviously striking and popular appeal, and it is probably largely on that account that his views have been so much neglected.

Yet he is one of the very few who have really succeeded in securing for education a clearly defined place in a philosophy of life, which is after all perhaps the most vital necessity for a true theory of education.

Lacking such definite philosophical relation to life as a whole, some of the most elaborate systems of instruction and organisation prove unsatisfying, and if Hegel had given us nothing more, we should at least be grateful for this, even supposing we do not wish to accept his philosophy in its entirety. For so many systems and views of education which are put forward are found on closer scrutiny to depend merely on tradition, personal bias, so-called practical necessity, or even on some one social, political or scientific position, that it is at least an intellectual relief to find the subject dealt with in its broad relations to life and the universe in general.

It might therefore be urged that Hegel wrote no special treatise on education, because the educational process was implied in his whole philosophy. Further, it may be said that his general philosophy can be clearly seen underlying all his pedagogic utterances, wherever they occur. Even in his school addresses, delivered to a mixed audience, consisting mainly of parents and pupils, no faltering or evasion can be noted, although he was dealing with subjects of instruction and discipline, before an unphilosophical audience. Their place and value are always considered from the standpoint of his fundamental philosophic beliefs and all his school work justified by reference to these.

Then again he dealt with what may be termed the

sociological aspects of education : the relations of the child and the school to society, involving, of course, on the one hand its connection with the family and on the other with the State.

This aspect of education is chiefly worked out in his Philosophy of Right, but is constantly referred to and amplified in other parts of his writings. To some extent at least he here breaks new ground, and opens up a field of inquiry which is proving of special interest in our own day.

In addition, he has also left valuable contributions to the pedagogy of secondary school education.

This is again an area too often left untouched, and in his time he was almost alone in his efforts to mark out the special province of secondary school work and to insist on its essential characteristics in regard to curriculum, method and discipline.

Of course Herbart and Froebel had no intention of confining themselves to elementary education, but it is obvious that they both lay chief stress on the earlier stages of development, and their main influence has been exerted in connection with the education of children under fourteen. Herbart, Basedow, Pestalozzi and Froebel were all pleading the cause of reform in the education given in elementary schools and lower stages of school work, but Hegel stands practically alone as the champion of distinctively secondary school education.

One cannot but be struck by Hegel's aloofness from contemporary educational thought. Many passages in his writings show that he was not unacquainted with the educational ideas and work of Rousseau, Pestalozzi,

Basedow, Bell, Lancaster and others, but he was obviously out of sympathy with their general views and uninfluenced by them in his own work. What he gives us, therefore, on the subject of pedagogy may be small in amount but it is emphatically his own and embodies at once his most fundamental philosophical principles and his actual teaching experience.

In these three directions at least then it may fairly be claimed that Hegel has made substantial, and in some ways unique contributions towards a theory of education. We must now, however, proceed with some care to consider each in turn, in order to estimate more exactly the nature of our indebtedness to him.

CHAPTER VII

HEGEL'S PHILOSOPHY OF LIFE IN RELATION TO EDUCATION

It is here necessary to endeavour to sum up very briefly the broad underlying ideas of the Hegelian philosophy of life, and to trace as far as we can their relation to his educational theory and practice. In order to do this as simply and clearly as possible we must always remember that Hegel was both an idealist and an evolutionist, also that in connection with these views he held that progress is only and always the result of the reconciliation of opposites — that advance is ever made through a process of antagonism overcome. When we say that Hegel's general philosophic standpoint was that of an idealist we mean that, according to his view, the only satisfactory interpretation of the universe is spiritual or mind interpretation. This implies that spirit or mind is the ultimate reality, but includes matter as a necessary part of its self-revelation in the universe. He distinguishes between the *natural* and the *spiritual*, but only as different parts of the same process. As an evolutionist he regards spirit as revealing itself unconsciously in the mineral world, rising through the vegetable to consciousness in the animal world and then attaining self-consciousness in humanity. Man therefore becomes the self-conscious arena of the final struggle between matter and spirit, whereof the victory, however long delayed, must be achieved by spirit and yet ultimately prove to be a conquest which does not destroy but fulfil.

Matter will in the end prove to have no meaning apart from spirit and should indeed be regarded only as a stage of spiritual evolution. Final reconciliation, or at-one-ment, will therefore be achieved and, her warfare being accomplished, the kingdom of the spirit at last must come.

In the history of the human race the story of this warfare is unfolded. Man only gradually becomes self-conscious, and passes out of the state of innocency, in which he was good, simply because he was one with nature guided by animal impulses and desires and knowing no higher law ; guiltless, in the sense that animals might be said to be guiltless when they work harm unknowingly. Through the long ages of human life on this earth man has worked his slow way up, gradually attaining with much painful effort some degree of mastery over himself and external nature. In this process intellectual and spiritual powers have evolved in him, his progress implying the gradual growth of will, its enlightenment and enfranchisement.

Such evolution is, however, slow and difficult, involving pain and evil. Indeed, in the early stages of growth it seems as if the only path of progress were through pain and evil.

Realities are only properly apprehended through contrast or opposition ; light has meaning only in opposition to darkness ; good in contrast with evil.

The spirit of the universe and of man is implicitly good, but that good can only be made explicit through experience of evil. Therefore it is through knowledge and experience of evil and pain that spirit can alone become self-consciously or morally good.

The fundamental difference between the natural and the moral, spiritual man is really one of freedom; the natural man is moved from without and has, properly speaking, no will of his own, but is the slave of natural conditions. The moral man commands himself and, having identified himself with the universal and the good, has attained true freedom.

A state of nature is a state of savagery and slavery. Freedom is nowhere to be found except in " the return of spirit through thought to itself, a process by which it distinguishes itself from the natural and turns back upon it."[1]

Still nature, no less than the spiritual world, is a revelation of God, but nature never becomes conscious of its divine essence. " Nature is a system of unconscious thought or to use Schelling's expression—petrified intelligence."[2]

This then is the path of evolution for humanity—to rise from the realm of nature to that of spirit, to pass from bondage to freedom, from the world of limitations to that of universals. But the process is no blind striving of the lower towards something higher which may be attained by chance. The motive force of evolution comes not from the material world, but from spirit. Spirit realising itself through matter gives purpose and

[1] VIII. 259.　　　　[2] VI. 24.

direction. The higher conditions the lower, the end
determines the means.

Now we have to think of this process of evolution as
going on both in the individual and in humanity as a
whole. The relations are reciprocal, the advance of one
depends largely on the advance of the other. Moreover, each human being born into the world tends
to reproduce in miniature the stages of development
through which the race has already passed; but the
experience and conquests of the past are the heritage of
the present, and these stages tend to be passed through
with greater and greater rapidity until that point is
reached from which further advance becomes possible
in each life.

Further, each individual has a threefold life as body,
soul and spirit, or perhaps it would be truer to say that
these represent three distinct planes of existence which
man must learn to live on and to control. The apparent
order of development of the individual is upward from
the body life, through that of the animal soul (instinct,
impulse, feeling, etc.) to the life of spirit (thought,
morality, religion, etc.). It has, however, already been
pointed out that, according to Hegel, the end determines
the process in evolution, and this holds good for the
individual as for the universe.

Account must be taken not only of development in
and from nature, but of that which conditions or determines nature. It is spirit desiring to express and
realise itself that becomes a living soul and takes on a
bodily form in order to gain experience and eventually
to attain a higher spiritual level. " The human form

is not, as is the animal, the body only of the soul, but also of the spirit." "Spirit, fulfilling its own law, determines to express itself in life and so to become at once both soul and physical existence. As living soul, the spiritual principle (Geistigkeit) of man fulfils the idea of the animal soul, by assuming a body." "However far above the merely living soul spirit may stand yet it makes for itself a body which appears to be organised and animated under the same conditions as the animal body." [1]

Thus spirit descends into matter, permeates and illumines it, so that the human body and soul are raised above the level of animal existence and made to subserve the higher life of the spirit.

It is now desirable to examine with some care the educational implications of Hegel's philosophic position. There is a certain classic simplicity in the broad outlines of his philosophy, and we can readily trace the same strong, simple lines, giving shape and form to his views on education. His idealism, and his belief in evolution, together with the special views he connected with the latter — e.g. progress by antagonism (involving self-estrangement and the gradual liberation of spirit)— determined in an unmistakable way all his statements concerning education, and we shall now proceed to consider the significance of his philosophy : (a) for the general concept of education ; (b) for the process and methods of education and instruction ; (c) in regard to the question of education values.

(a) Broadly speaking, it has already been made clear

[1] X. ii. 370.

that Hegel's philosophic position with regard to the
general concept of education was that of an idealist
and an evolutionist. The principle of the universe is
spiritual ; and man is one with the universe, although not
at first aware of this unity. Man as part of this evolving
unity is by nature progressive, but his own unaided
efforts will not carry him far. They need to be supplemented and indeed stimulated by the help of other
and more highly developed human beings. It is only
as he becomes possessed of intellectual and spiritual
powers that he begins to realise his unity with the
universe in which he lives. Until spirit is to some
extent set free from the bonds of the lower planes
of existence, it can do little to help itself. Education
then appears as a necessary part of the process of
realising this unity of the individual with the higher,
universal life, and is thus in a sense involved in the scheme
of evolution. For as in the human stage of the universe
evolution has to become self-conscious, it is clear that
human beings can and ought to share in this work and
become, as it were, co-workers with the universal spiritual
principle, so that thus the progress of evolution may be
promoted and hastened. Indeed it may be said that self-
conscious humanity owes it as a duty to each child born
into the world that he shall be placed under suitable
conditions of intellectual, moral and physical growth.

The position and work of the teacher is thus seen to
be of the utmost importance. The teacher is, as it were,
the reconciler under whose guidance the child is led to
unify his life, to overcome the antithesis between nature
and spirit.

To Hegel the term education always implied a liberation—a liberation of the spirit implicit in man from the
bonds of nature—and is to be effected largely by man's own
efforts, but in childhood and youth mainly through the
help of parents, teachers, books, and other influences.
This liberation implies the use of definite means—*e.g.*
instruction, discipline, etc., and the art of using these
means he terms pedagogy. "Pedagogy is the art of
making man moral : it regards man as one with nature
and points out the way in which he may be born again,
in which his first nature may be changed into a second
—a spiritual nature—in such a way that the spiritual
nature may become habitual to him." [1]

Morality is put as the end to be aimed at, because
the moral man, who has therefore identified himself
with the universal, is alone the free man. He held that
freedom is the essential quality of mind as weight is
of solid bodies. A truly liberal education, therefore, is
one which makes the mind free. The lower, natural,
or as we should perhaps say, animal mind, which is only
capable of dealing with the individual, the particular,
must undergo this change, this rebirth, by which it
becomes capable of comprehending the universal—of
living the life of the spirit.

The child begins life in a state of nature and innocency,
good only in a negative sense. " The child is implicitly,
by his nature, a rational being; but his reason is
merely potential in the shape of natural ability, of apti-
tude. This inner form is actualised—made explicit—
through education. The child does not realise his own

[1] VIII. 218.

inward nature and therefore in early years this must be developed by influences outside himself. He only realises that his parents, teachers and general environment demand something of him. The demand is from without and he obeys external authority. But through instruction and education his own inner powers are awakened and he becomes conscious that knowledge, morality and religion belong to his own nature. Education and instruction then aim at making him for himself—actually —what he is at first only potentially in the eyes of his parents and teachers." [1]

(b) We thus see the importance which Hegel attaches to education in general ; now let us examine a little more closely his views as to the process and methods of education, in the course of which it will also become clear why he laid such great stress on the importance of secondary education.

Evolution, according to Hegel, is not merely a natural or material process, it is rather a spiritual unfolding of which material development is but a phase, although a necessary condition, of the growing self-consciousness. In order to attain his full stature as an intellectual, moral and spiritual being, the individual must, on reaching a certain point in this development, break away, or, as it were, wrench himself free from his natural life, become self-estranged, and unite himself in thought with the universal life.   Thus he will learn to identify himself with universal law and order and to live in the world of ideas.   The full life of the community and the State then become possible to him as he breaks away from the

[1] VI. 278.

limitations of his purely natural individual life, loses himself to find himself once more in the great life of the world.

This stage in evolution must be regarded as a kind of second birth or initiation into a higher life. It is no peaceful process, no easy step to take, and many are those who do not take it at all, who never attain true manhood, but remain children all their lives. " Man is by nature the child, whose task consists in this—not to remain in this undeveloped merely potential condition, but to become explicitly what he is at first only implicitly—a free and reasonable being." [1] It is therefore just at this stage that the individual needs all possible help and encouragement from those who are further on than himself.

" This new birth of the spirit out of natural ignorance and error takes place through instruction and through that faith in objective truth and substance which is due to the witness of the spirit. This new birth of spirit is also one of heart." [2]

It is a stage that is usually reached during those years which coincide roughly with those of secondary school education, and is one that should specially occupy the attention of secondary school teachers. Unfortunately, " it is possible to remain in this state of childhood. The intellect and the will may remain through life in bondage to the natural man." [3]

It is this belief in the necessity for self-estrangement— of losing one's life to find it—of breaking away from the natural in order to become at home in the intellectual

[1] VI. 124.   [2] Introd. to *Encyclop*.   [3] VI. 275.

and the spiritual, that distinguishes Hegel's point of
view from that of others who have applied the idea of
evolution to education.

It also gives the clue to much that would otherwise
be obscure in his pedagogy.

As he deals almost entirely with education and instruction as carried on in a secondary school, we can understand how it is that he warns us so earnestly against
pandering too much to natural tastes. Effort is
necessary to strengthen the will, and the pupils must
learn to restrain their natural tastes and impulses and to
refrain from blindly following them. For these tastes
and impulses represent the natural man, which must be
left behind. Then, too, he urges that this is not the
period for sense training, but for the development of
the power of thought.

Now power of thought can only be attained by
practice in thinking. " Youth must first lose sight and
hearing, forego concrete presentation, withdraw himself
into the inmost night of the soul, in order to learn to see
on the mental plane, to grasp and to distinguish clearly
between intellectual conditions and ends." [1]

On the intellectual side the pupil must be thus led
out of himself into what seems at first a new world. He
must forget himself and become absorbed in a realm of
ideas not his own. " It is involved in the whole process
of education, that a man should gain his freedom from
the world of sensuous and direct forms by hard and long
endeavour and attain to the form of thought with its
appropriate simple expression." [2]

[1] XVII. 345.   [2] XVII. 345.

Hegel does not, however, mean to imply that this stage of self-estrangement is in any sense artificial; on the contrary it could only be effected in answer to some prompting from within. " This demand for separation is so necessary that it shows itself in us as a universal and well - known and recognised impulse." " The foreign, the far-off carries with it its own attractive interest, which compels us to work and striving and its value consists in its opposition to that which is near." " Youth considers it happiness to leave the familiar and with Robinson Crusoe to occupy a remote island. It is a necessary self-deception that depth must first of all be sought in the form of distance, but the depth and the power which we really attain, can only be measured in terms of distance from our own inner central point, that namely from which we started." [1]

Hegel calls this impulse " the centrifugal force of the soul."

It is clear, however, that this force left to itself may waste its energy : it needs guidance and direction. This then is the business of the teacher, to introduce the pupils to such subjects as shall afford scope for its action and at the same time subject it to such discipline as shall strengthen and support it. Hegel refers to what he calls a " partition wall by means of which this separation from self, so necessary for education, is effected."

By this he appears to mean that it is an absolutely necessary part of the process of self-estrangement that we shall realise that it has taken place. We must, as it were, both scale the wall and at the same time be quite

[1] XVI. First address.

sure that it is a wall. A language serves this purpose well, especially a dead language like Latin or Greek, which admits into a new world of ideas, which is also remote in time. A new terminology, such as we find in mathematics or a science, would serve the same purpose. But self-estrangement is only of value in view of the return journey, the rediscovery of the self in and as one with the universal.

"But this partition wall which separates us from ourselves, provides at the same time not only all starting points, but also those guiding lines which show the return path—the reconciliation of that which was opposed and the rediscovery of our real self, ours now in the light of the universal reality of spirit." [1]

It seems also clear that Hegel regarded this step of self-estrangement not only as a necessary step in the evolution of spirit but also as a condition of real acquirement, whether by memory, imagination or thought. In order to become objective, the material both of nature and of thought must be placed in opposition to us: they must assume the form of something strange and unfamiliiar. Even moral ideas can only thus be really made our own. "To have the concept of right, one must be educated to the stage of thinking, and not linger in the region of that merely which appeals to the senses."

It should, however, be noted that in the main this self-estrangement is an intellectual process only. The inner world of feeling is to be left undisturbed, nothing should be allowed to interfere with those "individual bonds

[1] XVI. First address.

which unite soul and spirit, feeling and thought in holy friendship with life, faith, love and trust." [1]

Hegel is often criticised for laying so much stress upon the necessity for a receptive attitude on the part of the pupil, but on closer study of his statements on this point it becomes obvious that he was referring almost entirely to this secondary school stage, when a passive, receptive, docile state of mind lends itself better than an active, self-assertive state would to the necessary conditions of self-estangement. " Like the will, thought must begin with obedience." [2]

When he refers with apparent approval to the rule of silence imposed upon the pupils of Pythagoras, it is clear that he had not little children in mind, but only those who were going on to develop a comparatively high degree of intellectual power. He is careful also to tell us that — " in order to receive, however, personal effort is needful, not in the form of original thought but as application of what has been learned ; as endeavour to bring it into right relation with other particular cases, and other concrete examples." [3]

It would seem to be a further implication of this general philosophical position that there are different stages of intellectual development and therefore certain necessary stages in intellectual education.

The first stage the child passes through is the natural, when things of sense hold sway and a warm, full, pulsating world of external nature lies around him.

This is the time for sense training, the encouragement

[1] XVI. First address.   [2] XVI. Second address.
[3] *Ibid.*

of self-activity, curiosity, imitation and creative effort, in order that the material world shall be fully realised and a firm foundation laid of facts and observations.[1]

In regard to this stage Hegel is silent, if we except some few references to elementary schools, for which he apparently approved "useful studies" and simple technical work, and his somewhat rigorous demand that some elements of Latin should be acquired early in order to save time in the secondary school.

He seems to assume that, given a good home, the child's early years should be spent there under the care of the mother, but it is pretty clear that he has little to offer in the way of suggestion as to the method of instruction at this stage. As it was Hegel's general practice to be silent on points regarding which he had not made up his mind, or upon which he had not reflected, there is no reason for any rash assumption on our part that he considered methods of instruction at the secondary school stage as equally suitable for little children.

In a second stage the child passes from under the absolute dominion of the world of nature and becomes capable of making himself a citizen of the world of ideas. This is of course the stage with which Hegel chiefly concerns himself and which we have already considered with some fulness.

A third stage is one in which the pupil approaching maturity, having gained intellectual power and entered into possession of himself, prepares for the service of humanity. He chooses his vocation and fits himself

[1] VIII. 90-100.

for it. This would correspond more nearly with the period of university than of school education, although perhaps at a gymnasium the introductory steps might be taken.

(c) In considering the claims of various subjects to a place in a secondary school curriculum, Hegel consistently views them in the light of his general philosophy of life. We shall later inquire more closely into his definite views on the value and mode of teaching some of these. Here it is sufficient to note that he always gave first place to those subjects which had most direct bearing upon the development of intellect and character. " So-called useful subjects," as he was apt to term them, must never be given precedence.

The classics, as offering best opportunities for self-estrangement and at the same time an almost endless store of noble thoughts and ideas ; moral and religious instruction, including the beginnings of philosophy, as affording guidance and inspiration at the same time as intellectual training ; these are the subjects which claim first attention, not that others are to be neglected, for balance must be maintained. Life is many-sided, and children must be prepared to take part in life, in the actual existing and not in a dream world. They must learn something about the natural world around them, and also their future vocations in life must not be lost sight of. With respect to the latter, however, it is pretty certain that Hegel considered that a thorough classical education made the best possible basis for every kind of professional work.

It was very fortunate that Hegel was able, on the whole,

to approve the general scheme of study laid down for the school; and that he and Niethammer were in such close sympathy in regard to the aims and means of education. Had it been otherwise, or if Hegel had been forced to lay chief stress on technical and commercial subjects, it is probable that his teaching experience would have come to a speedy end. For he was a man of strong, definite views, somewhat hard to move, and, for all his belief in the State, was not likely, even in her service, to change those of his views on education which were the direct outcome of his philosophy.

CHAPTER VIII

SOME DIFFICULTIES OF THE HEGELIAN POINT OF VIEW

IT has already been pointed out that perhaps the most valuable service that Hegel has rendered to education consists in the place he has given it in a philosophy of life.[1] We are led to view it, with him, not as something arbitrary and dependent on the will and caprice of individuals or of states, but as part of the necessary work of the universe, although a part the carrying out of which depends entirely on the co-operation of human beings with the divine principle in evolution. It thus assumes a dignity which nothing else can give it.

On the other hand, the very position thus given to education seems to involve the necessity for more light as to the ultimate meaning attached by Hegel to evolution in the individual and in the race. And just here it is that he leaves us in doubt as to his real views, supposing that he had indeed made up his own mind on this question. On the whole, it seems as if three alternative views were possible to one holding those philosophic positions which he has made clear to us.

According to the first the divine principle is a unity which seeks expression in ever-varying forms, of which

[1] VIII. 187. "Education is . . . an inherent element of the absolute, and is shown to have infinite value."

none, however—not even when expressed as the most
highly developed human being—has any permanence,
but each having played his brief part in a single life, slips
back into universal spirit, as a drop of water might slip
into the sea.

Or, secondly, the divine principle may be thought
of as differentiating itself for the purpose of full self-
realisation, and in this process developing independent
individualities which persist and yet eventually realise
their essential union with the divine, in which condition
individuality will not be lost but attain its full
significance. The " Rose Eternal " of Dante's vision,
whereof each petal, and even the position of each, had
meaning, gives this view in poetical form. According
to this view the divine principle immanent in the world,
and working up through the mineral, vegetable and
animal stages, would on attaining the human stage
of self-consciousness form permanent individualities ;
these then would need to pass through many lives
before the truly human being is evolved and the fully-
developed individual spirit becomes capable of realising
its unity with the divine. Spiritual union, involving,
not loss, but intensification of individuality and true
freedom, would thus be the goal of evolution. This
would of course involve the development of something
which we can only term cosmic consciousness, the
possibility of which is already being seriously considered by philosophers.

The third possible view is expressed in terms of
pluralism and supposes individual monads gradually
progressing towards perfection through a series of

successive lives, and at last reaching spiritual unity and becoming the divine—a unity made possible through the cementing power of love.[1]

It is obvious that Hegel's views will vary in significance according as one or other of the above interpretations of his use of the term evolution is adopted. In some ways the second of these interpretations seems to present fewest difficulties. On the one hand, if the divine principle is recognised as operative from the beginning—evolving matter as the necessary antithesis to spirit and then working up through all its grades to spiritual realisation—this makes the idea of definite purpose in evolution clearer than can be the case if we think of the progress of separate monads only. On the other hand, the evolution of permanent individualities, who yet are one with the divine in love and will and life, seems to be a more intelligible goal than the simple merging again into unity of those whose lives had been differentiated with so much care and effort. Nor is it easy to understand on this assumption how it is that there are such differences in the degree of evolution attained by persons often belonging to the same family; whereas if we assume the permanence of individuals, although progressing through a series of personalities, it is easy to realise that in the same time and part of the earth, even in the same family, we may have souls of different ages: some who after many lives have almost

---

[1] Of these views the first has been adopted by many German writers, amongst whom Feuerbach and Strauss may be mentioned, the second has recently been developed to some extent by Prof. Royce, while the third has been worked out by Dr M'Taggart.

won their freedom from the bondage of their lower nature, the slavery of their passions—while others have progressed but a little way on their journey upwards.

Viewed in this light, Hegel's doctrine of self-estrangement also falls better into place. He seems to regard this step as an absolutely necessary step in evolution, and yet on his own showing there are many who do not take it. Even if we leave women out of count—they having apparently, according to him, a different mode of progression—we yet realise that there must be numbers who either do not reach the stage or are not given the opportunity for taking it in one life.

Hegel is by no means as explicit as one could wish on the point. If the step is to be taken at about secondary school age, and especially if it needs such a special curriculum and mode of instruction as he seems to suggest in order that it may be fully accomplished, what will happen, it may well be asked, to those who cannot share in these advantages, those who have to be content with elementary schooling only or even those whose parents send them to a commercial or technical school at that critical age? On the whole it seems probable that he took here a similar view to that which he seems to hold about classes or ranks in society—viz., that human beings tend to gravitate towards that rank or estate in life for which they are by nature and development best fitted. It may be, therefore, that he assumed that those who were sufficiently evolved to profit by secondary school instruction would find it possible to get it. By his reference to bursaries and the like, we know that he considered that poverty should be no obstacle to a boy in getting secondary education if he showed by his ability and promise that he was likely to profit by it.

Of course the necessity for this self-estrangement step is much disputed; and, as it is pretty clear that all do not take it in the course of a single life we are driven to one of two conclusions. Either we must take the view just suggested, that human beings at any given moment are found to be at different stages of development—*i.e.* some are not ready for the step ; some are ready to take it ; and some seem as if they must have got beyond it. Or if we do not accept this view, we must hold that there are at least two different types of human beings —one that needs to take the step and one that does not.

In comparing men and women with regard to education, Hegel appears to adopt the latter, but on the other hand he never seems to distinguish two different types of men. It is of course true that he makes a distinction between educated and uneducated men, but the distinction he makes between men and women is not one of degree but of kind. "Women can of course be educated," he is careful to explain, but the process is different, no self-estrangement or progress by antagonism seems to be necessary in their case. " The education of women takes place one hardly knows how in an atmosphere of picture thinking as it were, more through life than through the acquisition of knowledge," whereas " man attains his position only through stress of thought and much specialised effort." [1]

He assumes that women have no " universal faculty ";

[1] VIII. 172.

but, as apparently this is only the possession of those men who have had it developed in them through education, one may fairly ask why he does not consider that definite secondary school education would be effective in their case too.   The only real answer is the one given above, that he regarded men and women as essentially different. Now he knew very little about the education of women ; and, as we know, in his day women had no higher and very little regular education at all, so he was not really in a position to judge of its possible effects.   On the contrary, those of us who have had to do with the education of girls at secondary school age are not likely to feel able to accept his view on this point.   It has certainly been the experience of most of us that many girls do go through a mental and spiritual change at that age ; that the step of self-estrangement is in many cases not only taken, but taken amid much intellectual and moral storm and stress. Moreover, in these days of university education for women, few would be prepared to endorse Hegel's dictum that their minds are not adapted to the higher sciences, philosophy or certain of the arts, " because these demand universality."   It is to be feared that Hegel tended sometimes to be a slave to his own philosophy.   He felt bound, for instance, to apply the idea of progress by antagonism or the reconciliation of opposites to every phase of life.   Consequently, amongst other things, his view of marriage had to be brought strictly into line ; and, man having been already described as a developing rational and universal being, woman had to be fitted into the plan as the opposite of this, and represented as having only unity of feeling but otherwise being the

sport of accidental inclinations and opinions.[1] If man
stands for spirit, then she must stand for nature, in order
that the reconciliation may be complete.

This brings us to another defect in his philosophy,
if it is to be regarded as a basis for educational theory—
its somewhat over-emphasis of the intellectual side of
mind. In the higher development of mind there seems
to be no room for feeling, and even will tends to be somewhat left out in the cold in respect of that second nature
which has become habitual.

It is true that he recognises the danger of relying too
much on habit instead of calling upon the will for fresh
efforts—"mere habit causes death," [2] but in regard
to feeling, he does not seem to realise any sense of loss.
Feeling and the emotions belong to the stage of childhood and the nature of women, but must apparently
be left behind by those who reach universality. The
State, he tells us, knows nothing of love, its sphere is the
sphere of law alone. Perhaps it is for that reason that
he dreads the participation of women in the service of
the State.[3] If it be indeed a true view of the State that
everything must be settled by hard reason, that love of
humanity, pity, mercy are to have no place, it is possible
that others besides women and little children would
prefer to remain without. No doubt Hegel did not
intend to push his views quite so far. He regarded a
developed morality as being able to accomplish all that
the love element in life could do, and without any uncertainty or possibility of variation. Still, from the
point of view of the educator, the hard intellectuality

[1] VII. 172.   [2] VIII. 151.   [3] VIII. 166.

of his views tends to limit their value and would do so more were it not that when Hegel comes to treat directly of educational practice he fortunately often fails to be consistent ; and the civil servant shows himself, for instance, to be the enthusiastic student of the classics, longing to lead his pupils into that enchanted land of beauty and to put them in sympathy with human hopes and fears and the great dramas of love and life and death. If literature were taught as he would have it taught, it could never be merely intellectual discipline, but must at the same time prove to be a training of the emotions of the finest kind.   Then again the personal interest he took in his boys, his efforts to cultivate their individual tastes and help each in the way that seemed to be needed at the moment ; his advocacy of physical exercises and drill, as aiding in the development of ready power of self-control ; these and other points in his practice all show that he was able to transcend the apparent limits of his theory, and perhaps indeed that these limits tend to disappear in view of a wider interpretation of his philosophy. For it is very striking that these limits are chiefly, if not entirely, apparent in those domains of thought to which he had given but scanty attention ; and it is perhaps hardly fair to lay great stress on his few recorded utterances in connection with questions he had not properly faced, and in which perhaps he was not specially interested.

We are apt, no doubt, to ask too much of any one human being, however great he may be. The great philosopher gives us the broad foundations for educational theory ; but he cannot be at the same time expected to work out all its details and application. Life is too short for this, even if it could be shown—which is more than doubtful—that the epoch-making thinker is at the same time the one best fitted to guide the practical working out of his views to successful issue, in all the many possible directions of their application.

Where, however, Hegel did put his views into practice in the secondary school, he was singularly successful; and although the field of his teaching work was limited, it is one that presents very special difficulties. His success gives, in fact, a happy augury of what might be expected from a careful working out of these implications of his philosophy in other spheres of education. Hegel has had many followers, but few real interpreters in this direction, and it may be that the Hegelian school of educational thought has yet to be founded.

The work of Rosenkranz and of Froebel must not be forgotten; but the former has had no far-reaching influence, and the latter has tended to be valued rather for his practice than his theory. There has, of course, been much written in Germany, especially about the middle of the nineteenth century, on Hegel in relation to education; but in most instances it is difficult to avoid the suspicion that his views are being used as a kind of stalking horse, behind which the writer's own views are being pushed forward.

The Hegelian philosophy, unfortunately, by its very comprehensiveness, lends itself to this device; as it is possible to find something in it to support almost any views, if sufficient care be exercised in selection. At

F

the present moment educational theory is sorely in need of some satisfactory philosophic basis. In our country at least practice has outrun theory and much good work in education is being done which we feel to be right and desirable, but which we hardly attempt to justify on general grounds. We are apt to urge instead, that such and such a subject is useful and to talk vaguely about training character; but comparatively few have any settled or satisfying policy in respect of education. To many, of course, the Herbartian philosophy appeals; but for the large and increasing number of those who fail to find full satisfaction therein, it may be that the Hegelian philosophy will be found to provide that which they have vainly sought elsewhere.

CHAPTER IX

THE SOCIOLOGICAL ASPECTS OF EDUCATION

THE FAMILY, THE SCHOOL AND THE STATE, AND THEIR
RELATIONS TO THE CHILD AND TO EACH OTHER IN
RESPECT OF EDUCATION

THE term "child" is always apt to be somewhat vague
and it may be well to consider more closely the sense or
senses in which Hegel uses it. Strictly speaking, he
distinguishes between two well-marked stages in the
development of the young.[1] To the first of these he
applies the term childhood and to the second youth.
Childhood is the period when the child's mind is wrapped
up in itself—in unity with nature. Youth is the time
of the " developed antithesis," in which his immediate
individuality opposes itself to the stress and influence of a
universality which is still only subjective (as shown in
ideals, fancies, hopes, ambitions).

Hegel here seems clearly to mean that childhood is
the period for early education in the family or elementary
school, while by youth he indicates more precisely the
secondary school age. But unfortunately he tends to
use the terms: the child, the pupil, the young and
youth, somewhat indiscriminately when referring to
education; and this too often results in a certain

[1] VII. ii. 87, 88.

ambiguity. In any case of doubt, however, we shall probably interpret him rightly if we do so in the light of his general philosophical position. Here at least is no ambiguity, and with this guide most of our difficulties will disappear.

The Family and the Child.—The family is always regarded by Hegel as an institution which expresses the direct or natural ethical spirit. The unity of the family is one of feeling, the feeling of love, which is the ethical in the form of the natural.[1] The ethical principle of the family " is actually realised in the second or spiritual birth of the children—in educating them to independent personality." [2]

The education of the young thus assumes a position of prime importance in the family, and may be regarded as its chief function. The child then belongs to the family and has a right to be supported and educated by the parents. His relation to his parents is " a personal relation, one of feeling, of love, of natural faith and trust." In the child the parents' love is objectified " in a spiritual being, in whom the parents are loved, and whom they love." [3] " The child is of value because he is the child ; he receives the love of his parents without merit on his part, so also he has to endure their anger without the right to resent it." [4]

The child has certain rights and also certain duties, and it is the same on the part of the parents. As " children are potentially free, and life is the direct embodiment of this potential freedom," they cannot be

[1] VIII. §§ 157, 158.   [2] VIII. § 521.   [3] VIII. 174.
[4] VIII. 120.

regarded as property either that of the parents or of the community. But their freedom is as yet only potential. It is with children as it is with " nations under paternal government—the people are supplied with food . . . and are not regarded as self-dependent or of age. Because of weakness and immaturity, the child must be dependent on others for his bodily needs and for due education and training. Man does not possess by instinct what he is to be, but must first of all acquire it. Upon this is based the child's right to be educated." [1] On the other hand he must show trust and obedience. Hegel is very emphatic as to the importance of exacting absolute unquestioning obedience in early years. The little child, he thinks, is not influenced by ideas and reasons, and therefore to reason with a child is useless, and by doing so you also make him realise the possibility of disobedience. To the child its parents stand for the universal, and obedience rendered to them is training for future obedience to moral law. The child is at first non-moral and can only become moral through education, by means of which the child may become fit to exchange obedience to external authority—parents and teachers —for a higher form—namely, obedience to his higher self as one with universal law and order. In regard to this point Hegel tells us, " children have no moral will but are guided by their parents," [2] and again " children . . . are completely or almost completely, irresponsible for their actions." [3]

The rights of the parents are thus seen to be really limited to education and to whatever else may promote

[1] VIII. 174.   [2] VIII. 107.   [3] VIII. 120.

the good of the child. The child is not a slave and
therefore the parent has not even a right to his services
if in any way such services would tend to hinder rather
than help development. In any case such service should
only be required in the common interest of the family.

The parents, it is true, have the right to punish, not
in the interest of abstract justice as such, but in order
to impress on the child the necessity for restraining that
" natural will " which is opposed to the content of
freedom. " The child, or uneducated man, possessing
only natural will, is not fully responsible." Correction
is indeed an important part of its parents' duty, merely
natural impulses and self-will must not only be restrained
but even eradicated.[1]

Hegel's view of punishment is striking and suggestive,
in that he urges its importance not because it is justifiable
either as a preventive or retributive measure, but because
it is the right of the child or indeed of any wrongdoer.

It is because the child (or other morally undeveloped
person) is potentially moral and rational that he has
this right to punishment. Pain in some form seems to
be an essential of progress, and even in respect to the
child it is to some extent true to say that " knowledge
by suffering entereth," that pain and hardness mark the
way by which alone human beings attain the higher
life—viz., that conditioned by universal moral, intellectual and spiritual laws. As this higher life is the
really human life and implicit in the child, punishment
is simply a way of forcibly calling his attention to it,
helping him to realise his true inner nature, which has

[1] VIII. 139.

been temporarily obscured by his lower animal impulses. It thus appears almost as a necessary mode of moral instruction, and parents neglect their duty and retard the moral evolution of the child if they fail to punish when necessary.

Hegel suggests that the child feels his incompleteness and is dissatisfied with what he is. He has an " impulse to belong to the world of adults whom he reverences as higher beings." He desires to grow up, to become big, and if not kept well in hand may become forward and impertinent. Yet the sense of subordination, so important at this stage of the child's development, is to be induced, not by fear, but by that love and reverence which causes him to look up to his parents as superior to himself and gladly to submit to their guidance. The real ground of his obedience will then be the only true one—recognition of actual superiority.

" It has ceased to be the custom in the family . . . to induce in children a feeling of subjection and bondage— to make them obey another's will even in unimportant matters—to demand absolute obedience for obedience' sake and by severity to obtain what really belongs alone to the feeling of love and reverence and the gravity of the case in question."

At first sight a certain amount of contradiction appears to be involved in Hegel's insistence on the importance of correction and punishment (which seems to be connected with the idea of law) in the family—which he regards as the sphere of love. This contradiction is, however, more apparent than real, although Hegel indeed tells us himself that " it is easier to love children than to train them." Yet if we regard love as ethical in its nature, that surely implies some purpose or end to be realised, and in the case of the child this must be the child's good—which it has already become clear is not momentary pleasure or avoidance of pain, but that which promotes his spiritual progress. Then we must remember that he is not advocating harshness or severity, and also that there are degrees even of pain and punishment. It is pretty certain that Hegel did not contemplate the infliction of more than is necessary.

It may be noted that he does not anywhere allude to corporal punishment, and it is probable that the pain of thwarted wilfulness and of restraint generally was what he chiefly had in mind. He says that " the more children are inclined to disobedience and wayward wilfulness, the more one must continue to command them." A firm, but loving control of conduct, supplemented, when found necessary, by punishment, carefully adapted to the end of bringing home to the growing self-consciousness the supremacy of universal law and order, and of course in early years the supremacy of the parents, as standing objectively for that law and order—is probably what he had in mind.

Very slight correction—a word, a look—may be sufficient punishment under some circumstances, and a child brought up in an atmosphere of love may be even more sensitive to such than the hardened criminal would be to fairly severe treatment. For unfortunately it is possible that evil may become second nature instead of good, and in dealing with the criminal we have to do with more than the waywardness of the original nature.

Through habitual giving way to them, the lower impulses have usurped the place of the higher moral self that should have been developed. The task which punishment has to accomplish is then harder, and in order to have its due effect the pain it causes must be greater in proportion. The lighter punishments given in youth save pain and trouble in the end, and love in the true interest of the child will not withhold them.

Hegel tells us that education in the family has a twofold aim. On the one hand there is the direct aim of laying the foundations of moral life in the child by developing love, trust and obedience and generally a right attitude of mind towards all that is good and right. On the other hand, by gradually helping the child to develop a free personality and a certain measure of independence, the family prepares him for the wider life of the world.

The responsibility for this early stage of training Hegel assigns mainly to the mother, especially that part of it which relates to that right-feeling attitude which he regards as the true starting point of all morality and social life

He has nothing to say about any formal instruction in reading or other subjects before the child goes to school; but it seems probable that he contemplated that some would be given in view of his somewhat scathing remarks on " teaching in play " (*spielende Pädagogik*)[1] which he makes while still treating of education in the family. He urges, and quite rightly, that children take themselves and life somewhat seriously,

[1] VIII. 175.

and that they resent any attempts to make fun of or treat lightly that which they know to be serious. At the same time, as we shall endeavour to make clear elsewhere, Hegel failed to realise that play has two meanings, and that in one of them it represents by no means a frivolous, but rather a serious mode of representation of life on the part of the child.

Family life really terminates from an ethical point of view when each child belonging to it has developed an independent personality and attained his majority, but long before the termination of this stage of human development, another influence—that of the school—has come into the life of the child. To a consideration of that important institution and sphere of influence we must now turn our attention.

The Child and the School.—Hegel appears to regard the school as the necessary complement of family life, and at the same time as affording a means of transition from the narrow family round of life and interest to the broad, many-sided life of the world.

As the child is potentially a social being he must be gradually trained to live the social life in the first place in the family circle, with its simple relationships, and then in the school, which provides him with a new set of social conditions in preparation for real life.

Rousseau's idea of educating Emile, apart from all social influences, by himself, under a tutor instead of in a school, he considers to be thoroughly unsound and even impracticable.[1]

The ideal school for Hegel is the day school and

[1] VIII. 153.

indeed, except for orphans, he does not seriously contemplate any other kind. He seems, on the whole, to believe that the division of the child's life between the school and the home is of special educational value in helping the child to understand himself, and in preparing him for the future necessity, when grown up, of rightly holding the balance between public and private life.

The child then begins to realise upon first entry into school life that he may be considered from two points of view: from that of family affection (which does not necessarily imply that he is in himself valuable or even lovable), and also from that of his teachers and comrades at school—from which standpoint all depends upon himself. In the latter case he will only count for something and be esteemed and liked if he has or can develop the necessary intellectual, moral and even physical qualities. He must earn his position, for no one will take him on trust. Further, he learns that all-important lesson of co-operation with his equals, both in work and play.

The importance of law and order is brought home to him through school discipline and its rewards and punishments. But above all for Hegel the school is "a sphere of work mainly concerned with ideas and thought." [1]

Here it is that the world "of inner treasure which parents give their children through a good education and proper use of schools" is opened to them. These inner treasures "are incorruptible and preserve their value under all circumstances." A good education is the best and surest possession which parents can give

[1] XVI. Third address.

and bequeath to their children.[1] The child is implicitly rational, as well as moral, and it is in the school that he must learn to think and reason, as well as to be trained and disciplined. Hegel distinguishes somewhat between the work of an elementary and a secondary school. " Secondary schools are mainly places of instruction, not directly of training or discipline." " But though the school presupposes early moral training, yet moral education is in immediate connection with its chief business of instruction." [2]

We have elsewhere considered Hegel's very important view that in the secondary school the step of self-estrangement has chiefly to be secured.

The School and the Family.—The relation of the school to the family is obviously both close and important, and Hegel again and again urges the necessity for co-operation between them. If the family does not do its share of the work, and also support the authority of the teachers in regard to their share, the school and therefore, of course, the child, must suffer.

" The school is the intermediate stage, which leads man from the family circle into the world," [3] and therefore it must have close connection both with the family and with the community.

Hegel thinks it very necessary to define the respective spheres of the home and the school in order to prevent undue interference with each other, but he also believes that each institution gains by being required to concentrate on certain aspects of the child's life and work.

---

[1] XVI. Fourth address.   [2] XVI. Second address.
[3] XVI. Third address.

In matters of instruction the school takes precedence, but it is for the home to secure proper conditions for private study out of school hours.

As regards discipline, the school is only directly responsible during school hours. The family must primarily undertake all outside control. Hegel is very emphatic on the point, that the school must not be blamed for home neglect. Yet of course he recognises that the pupil is not and should not be regarded as two different persons, one in the school and another outside, so that both home and school have really the greatest interest and a good deal of indirect influence in each other's spheres. Believing that, as compared with teachers, "parents stand in closer relation to the circle of their children's conduct, and children more easily relate to them what takes place at school or in connection with it, they can hear much which is carefully hidden from the attention of the teacher," Hegel earnestly requests the parents of his pupils, in one of his school addresses, to give information to the teachers when any unbecoming behaviour on the part of the pupils comes under their notice. The teachers would be greatly indebted to them, as often it is only in this way that the school can be put into a position to check the mischief, and to remove any injurious influence at work among the children; thus also they will be enabled to co-operate with the parents, for it is through common and united action alone that anything can really be accomplished in the case of serious and especially of moral faults.[1]

In one important passage Hegel brings out what he

[1] XVI. 158.

considers to be an essential difference between home
and school education, or rather, it might be said, between
home and early education taken together and education
at the secondary school stage. In the family, as we have
seen, the child's individuality is of importance and
should be taken account of as long as he is in the stage
of childhood. But when he reaches the next stage—
that of youth—this step implies that he has to realise
universality; then, says Hegel, "one ought not to estimate
individuality too highly. Rather must we consider
as mere empty words and wide of the mark, the assertion
that the teacher should devote himself carefully to the
individuality of the pupil and study and cultivate it.
He has no time for this. In the family circle the child's
idiosyncrasies are tolerated ; but with the school begins
a life according to general law and order, under arrangements common to all. There the mind must be brought
to relinquish its peculiarities and to make his own what
is common (or well known) knowledge, and the will of the
majority; and to submit himself to the usual mode of
instruction. This transformation of the mind and this
alone is worthy of the name of education. The more
cultivated a man is the less does one see in his behaviour
anything peculiar or out of the way." [1]
Now this statement has often been taken to mean
that, according to Hegel, individuality is worthless—
that the nature of ideal man is absolute and invariable,
and can only be attained at the cost of eliminating all
individual peculiarities   This is far from being his real
view, which is rather that true individuality is sacred, and

[1] VII. ii. 82.

only its excrescences and peculiarities must be got rid of. This misunderstanding has probably arisen in two ways.

In the first place, it may arise by taking the above passage away from its context. Examined in the light of its context, we find that Hegel expressly recognises that human beings differ, that some have talent in one or more directions and that some have genius in varying degrees, and that even with regard to character human beings differ, not because of education but on account of some original difference in nature; and he does not suggest that this implies some radical mistake in the constitution of the universe—which we should endeavour to counteract in education.

In the second place, it is probably the result of forgetting that when Hegel speaks of the school it is almost always the secondary school he has in mind, and that, according to him, this represents the stage in evolution when the universal has to be realised and assimilated. During this stage the individuality is to be kept as far as possible in the background in order that the higher universal self may be developed. Still, the work is after all with individuals, for, as he says elsewhere: " The sphere of education has to do with individuals only, its aim is to bring the universal mind to birth in them." [1] When that higher self has gained strength and stability, then is the time to unite it with those individual char- acteristics which belonged to his original nature; and in the strength of this reconciliation the man, now really human, will go forth into the world to perform that special work for which he is fitted both by nature and education.

[1] VII. ii. 31.

THE CIVIC COMMUNITY AND THE STATE IN RELATION TO
THE CHILD AND THE SCHOOL

Although Hegel distinguishes carefully between the
civic community and the state, it will yet be convenient
for us to consider them together in their relation to
education.

The civic community is regarded by him as intermediate between the family and the state.

While the family represents an ethical unity, the civic
community shows us diversity—*i.e.* individuals (and
families) adjusting themselves to each other and combining in order to secure the necessaries of life and
conditions of safety, law and order. A certain universality is present, in that it is the common good that
is aimed at ; but it needs to be attained in each direction.
Civic society is then " the developed totality of this
system of adjustments and relations."

The State is, however, " the self-conscious ethical
substance, the unification of the family principle with
that of civil society," or " the realised ethical idea,"
" freedom actualised." It must be regarded as the
national, universal political constitution, under which
city and country, families and persons, find themselves
united.

The State, therefore, is regarded by Hegel as " the
higher authority in respect to which the laws and interests
of the family and civic community are subject and
dependent."

Yet it is the civic community that must arrange and

carry out the general policy of the state, and therefore in regard to education Hegel tends to speak rather of the community than of the state, although it is fairly evident that he considered the state as the force in the background — the necessary support and sanction of local effort. The state gives the reason and justification of all civic duty—" the citizen discharges his duty as State business."

Youth, according to Hegel, is affected very greatly by the state to which he belongs. He quotes with approval the answer of the old Greek philosopher to a father who consulted him as to the best way to bring up his son : " Make him a citizen of a state that has good laws," [1] and in the same connection urges that " only when the individual is a citizen of a good state does he receive what is due to him." [2]

In the gradual advance of civilisation the individual has ceased to be merely the son of the family ; he " has become the son of the community, which makes claims upon him, while at the same time he also can claim rights from it." [3]

The community in its own interest, as well as for the sake of the child, requires that he shall be educated. If the family cannot provide such education, or can only provide it in part, the community must supersede or supplement the family effort. As also it is recognised that school education is on the whole necessary and best for the majority—the provision of schools is also a civic matter. The community has " in its character of universal family, the right and duty of undertaking the

[1] VIII. 261.   [2] VIII. 153.   [3] VIII. 238.

G

superintendence and carrying out of education—even against the parents' wishes—at least in so far as the production of efficient members of society is concerned." "Likewise to make arrangements for the provision of suitable educational institutions." [1]

Hegel owns that it is very difficult to define exactly the respective scope and limits of parental and civic responsibility. He points out that too often parents assume that they have the sole right to decide whether a child shall be educated or not, and in any case what shall be the mode of his training; they resent therefore any interference. It is just here that the laws of the state support the community in its endeavour to secure the rights of the child, as a member of the community, to education and moreover to the right kind of education. Not only where the parents entirely neglect their duty, but where through ignorance, poverty or other cause the child is not likely to get what is needful, the community has a right to step in. Compulsory education is thus necessary, and no parent has a right to resent the child being forced to attend any school in which the organisation, methods employed, etc., are such as are commonly approved.

The community and the state owe a duty to themselves as well as to the child and the family, and this duty is that of securing that there will be in the future a sufficient supply of suitably trained and educated men to carry on the necessary civil and political work. Hegel considers that "public educational institutions are pre-eminently nurseries for civil servants and they

[1] VIII. 239.

owe this responsibility to the government—not to supply it with incapables."[1] It follows further from this position that everything connected with school arrangements—discipline, methods, subjects, instruction, and even the promotion of boys from class to class, must always be regarded in the light of this responsibility to the state. He has a good deal to say on this aspect of the question in his school address of the year 1813. In it he tries to make clear to the parents of his boys that ultimately the interests of the family and the state are really the same. Parents, no doubt, would desire to see their sons promoted quickly, pressed forward in their studies and finally selected and advised to take up certain professions. But he very rightly points out that it would be mistaken kindness to press and promote quickly a boy whose capacity and stage of development did not warrant this; the result could only be disappointing both to the family and the community; and the boy himself would suffer, be discouraged, and also retarded instead of advanced in his course of development.

He appeals to what he knows must be the parents' desire as citizens—" to have as spiritual advisers and as preachers those who possess the authority which comes from spiritual insight and uprightness; skilled physicians for the care of their bodily needs, and that the public weal should be in the hands of sensible and honest men," as a reason why they should not demand that their sons, if found unfit, " should be pushed on towards such professions and offices of the State."

The school no less than the pupils must consider

[1] XVI. Second address.

itself as subordinate to the community and the state; not only so, it must even regard itself as expressing the will and requirements of these towards the child. The boards of studies and the teachers as well as the parents must subordinate their wishes to these higher conditions. The teachers must feel themselves to be real civil servants and bound to carry out faithfully and punctually the work entrusted to them.

Hegel does not seem to be in favour of private schools. He considered that they could not have the same authority and influence as public schools, that they were unlikely to be as well conducted and equipped, and especially, that they would be characterised by an individual and particular, instead of a social and universal spirit.

At a time when Fichte was calling upon the German people to establish Pestalozzian schools, and when those of the type of the Philanthropinum and other particular kinds were being viewed with much popular favour, Hegel urges his countrymen not to follow this or that private leader in education but to put upon the state and the community the duty of working out their own salvation in matters educational, in full trust that their confidence would not be misplaced.

CHAPTER X

THE SECONDARY SCHOOL CURRICULUM

ACCORDING to Hegel the aim of the school determines its curriculum. Decide first what the school is intended to accomplish, and then choose your tools and materials for building, seems to have been his general advice on this important question.

The number of years which the pupil will spend in the school is of course one of the determining factors in the matter. For those who must leave at the earliest possible age—*i.e.* those generally who form the majority of elementary school pupils—the curriculum must include the necessary everyday kind of knowledge which each human being should possess about his country, people, and natural surroundings, religion, the necessary instruments for obtaining these (*i.e.* speech, reading, writing, etc.), and such training as shall ensure the foundation of good habits and a right attitude towards life, this training being the result partly of the moral atmosphere of the school, including the good example of the teacher. Home influence should not only supplement this training but must initiate all that appertains to good behaviour and right feeling. But all this instruction and training absolutely necessary as they are indeed, do not constitute what Hegel regarded as education in the fullest sense. Exercising the senses, and by their means becoming acquainted with phenomena of the material world—learning useful facts and arts—are the preliminaries of education, but not the real process itself. As we have already seen, education in the true sense meant for Hegel liberation of the human spirit from the world of merely sense impressions, and making possible the higher life of the mind on intellectual and spiritual planes. As this is a somewhat slow process, and as indeed it would seem to imply that the earlier period in which the developing senses required exercise was in large measure past—it is clear that many years of school life are necessary if both the preliminary training and real education are to be accomplished. It was therefore to the secondary school, and especially to the type which leads on to the university, that Hegel looked to show the real educational process at work.

In his first annual address delivered at the Nürnberg Gymnasium in 1808, he makes a great point of trying to distinguish clearly the relative functions of different types of schools. Considerable alterations had just been brought about in the schools of Nürnberg and a general adjustment of the whole educational system was taking place. No doubt the popular mind was still a little vague as to what had really been done, and as to the respective functions of the different kinds of schools which were being established or developed.

Hegel, therefore, not only tried to make clear the special function and curriculum of the gymnasium, but made an effort to bring home to the people of Nürnberg the existing educational facilities of which they might avail themselves.

First, in reference to the elementary schools, he points out that the Government has, " through the completion of the elementary school system, widened the general education of the community ; in these schools all may learn that which is essential to them as human beings and useful for their condition in life." Next, he proceeds to consider the provision made for secondary education, distinguishing carefully between the two different types of schools in which this may be secured. One important school of each kind was to be found in Nürnberg, the Real Institut and the Aegidiengymnasium, of which he was rector.

The first of these provided a curriculum intended to meet the needs of those who were destined for business and commercial pursuits, in preparation for which the sciences and technical subjects were of chief value. It does not seem to have been intended to serve as an avenue to the university (where indeed the study of science had not yet attained any real importance) and the training it afforded on the literary side consisted mainly in the study of national literature, history, and modern languages.

Hegel is naturally reticent in his references to what he terms this sister establishment, and it is not quite easy to ascertain his real views with regard to the type of curriculum for which it stood. He seems to have frankly recognised the need for such schools and to have realised their value and importance for the State. In speaking of the organisation of education and the necessity for different types of schools, he urges that a certain amount of separation and limitation is essential, and that "the true sign of the freedom and strength

of an organisation consists in this—that the different
elements which compose it shall fit into each other and
make a complete system, carrying on their work side by
side without envy and without fear—as parts of one
great whole." [1]

We shall also see later that he was really interested
in the study of science and a believer in the study of
national and contemporary languages and literatures
as far as they went, although it is obvious that he considered the range of vernacular literature as too limited
to be completely satisfactory.   It is probable, however,
that he regarded the development of technical training
at secondary school age with more distrust, fearing, no
doubt in view of the growing interest which it excited,
that it might come to occupy too large a place in popular
estimation.   Technical training tends to concentrate
attention on those more material aspects of life which
are connected with earning a livelihood and getting on
in the world, and this implies, at least to some extent,
keeping personal interest to the fore.   Now this can
only be allowed with safety after the character is at least
to some extent formed, after the boy has lost himself to
find himself, and gained his freedom from the bondage
of the senses.   Over-insistence on the useful aspects of
instruction would, he feared, not only leave no time for
liberal education,—the true secondary school work,—but
might even militate against it.

It is no doubt with this in mind that he presses upon
his countrymen the importance of securing for as many
as possible that kind of education which results in the

[1] XVI. First address.

development in each of " a central core of independent
worth, of purposive ends, which forms the first foundation of all after usefulness in life, and which it is important
to cultivate in the minds of those belonging to all ranks
of society."

He refers to other countries which " neglected and
despised attempts to secure and develop in the minds
of the people any such inner characteristics, confining
their attention merely to useful subjects " ; and suggests
that these have availed them nothing in the time of their
distress.   In danger and difficulty it is character that
tells and not many " useful devices."

In any case it is clear that the type of secondary
education with which he was in real sympathy was that
provided at the gymnasium, of which he had become
rector.

This gymnasium was a classical secondary school
of the new kind, in which, although the classics occupied
the first place in the curriculum, room was left for the
study of other important subjects.

It is also necessary to note that in this—and in similar schools established mainly under the influence of
Niethammer—the classics were to be studied not merely
for the sake of scholarship, but for their bearing on life
and character.   These schools were in no sense mere
revivals of that of Sturm and of others of the later
Renascence period, they were rather of the broad,
humanist type of the early Italian movement.   It was
the Greek ideal of free, harmonious life which Vittorino
da Feltre had in his day tried to realise in the Mantuan
school, not the Jesuits' standard of Ciceronian perfec-

tion of style and scholarship, which caused Hegel to throw himself so enthusiastically into Niethammer's schemes for the reform of classical schools. It followed too that Hegel was not simply interested in the classical work of the school. He eagerly welcomed every subject in turn that might help to give his pupils entrance into the world of thought and awaken their mental activity there. To the experiment of introducing simple philosophical teaching into the school he naturally gave most careful attention, but he was almost equally solicitous about other subjects, even those to which he would not have felt so directly attracted.

As the subjects included in the curriculum of his school have been given elsewhere, as well as an extract from Niethammer's Normativ, it will now only be necessary to bring together such of Hegel's views and teaching methods in regard to various studies and school exercises as we can discover in his writings.

Most of his expressed views can, however, be grouped conveniently round two subjects—viz.: (*a*) Classics, and (*b*) Religious, Moral and Philosophic Instruction. Language teaching in general, grammar, etc., obviously connect with the former, while the latter will no less clearly include the consideration of a group of subjects.

In respect of certain subjects, such as mathematics and science, we have little to go upon. We know that Hegel was interested in mathematics and that he taught the subject, at least for a time. With regard to science, we know from his writings that the theoretical side at least had very real value in his eyes; moreover, that he was accustomed to devote a part of his course of moral and philosophic instruction to a consideration of the significance and value of each of the chief sciences; further, that he did all he could to encourage the introduction of more practical science work in his school, and that in spite of the fact that it was essentially a classical school.

Finally, it has been found possible to put forward his views on such matters as military exercises, methods of study, etc., in his own words and these extracts from his writings will be found in the appendix.

CHAPTER XI

THE VALUE AND METHODS OF CLASSICAL STUDIES

BEFORE attempting to formulate Hegel's positive views on the place and importance of classical studies, it will be well to distinguish, as far as possible, his general position from those held by some of his predecessors or contemporaries with whose views it might be compared.

His general position has already been broadly indicated as showing many points of resemblance with that held by early Italian humanists. When he tells us of the wonder and beauty of the " Golden Age," of its noble ideas of life and conduct and the superlative value of classical literatures as means of liberal education, we might almost fancy ourselves transported to Italy in the early fifteenth century and listening to one of the great humanist teachers in that first bright morning of the Renascence.

The words of Vergerius, "We call those studies *liberal* which are worthy of a free man ; those studies by which we attain and practise virtue and wisdom," [1] might have been used by Hegel himself. For Hegel too the ideal of the " free man " was ever present—the man to whom the realms of intellectual and moral ideas lie

[1] " De Ingenuis Moribus."

open ; the man who, making these ideas his own, drawing
them, as it were, into himself, endeavours to realise them
concretely through his life as a citizen.   But close as is
the likeness between the Hegelian and humanistic
positions, it will be seen that they were not quite parallel ;
that even the terms " free " and " liberal " studies
are not used in exactly the same sense.

In later Renascence times, we know that the ideal of
education narrowed.   No longer the citizen, but the
scholar, even the stylist, came to be regarded as the
finest product of the school and university.   With the
exclusiveness of this aim Hegel had little sympathy.
Few have indeed appreciated more than he the beauty
of literary form to be found in classical literature, but
it was more to the bearing of the study of that literature
upon life, and therefore to the subject matter, that he
attached real educational significance and value.   It
is true he held that those great intellectual and moral
ideas could not be fully made our own through translations, and that therefore the languages in which they
were expressed must be mastered ; but a study of language
alone would never have appeared to him as affording a
liberal education.

Nor did he feel the need of a universal language, which
led Comenius and others to labour in the direction of
simplifying the learning of Latin and adapting it to
modern requirements.

The carrying out of the Pansophic scheme required a
universal language, in order that scientific achievements
should be made useful and accessible to all ; and Latin
appeared to Comenius, if not the language best adapted

for the purpose, at least the only one available. In this case, however, Latin was studied entirely with a useful end in view. Not the literature, but the language was needed; and the language not as valued by the Ciceronian for its beauty and fitness of form, but as an aid to the advancement of knowledge. While the effect of Ciceronianism through concentration upon the strict study and use of the language was to limit ideas to those of ancient life and thought, in fact to revive the past, Comenius looked to the future and to the introduction of new ideas as all important. His ideal kingdom was yet to come, and Latin was only a medium for the propagation of ideas.

It might be said that Hegel, like Comenius, looked to the future, not to the past, for the development of ideal society; but he regarded the classical literatures—and Greek literature even more than Latin—as a storehouse of noble human thought, valuable for all time; and a storehouse upon which we must draw at least such material as may be necessary to lay a firm foundation for the building of the temple of ideal humanity. Yet it is probably more true to say that Hegel's real hope and interest lay, not in the past or the future, but in the present. The past was of value inasmuch as it afforded light and training for the present, and the future as its outcome. But the educator has to deal with the problem of to-day, and to that must his best strength be given.

Hegel had still less in common with Basedow and his philanthropic friends, who taught Latin through games and other devices and sought to make it the means of expression for everyday ideas and needs.

They desired to give it the position of a common, universal language, not only for the purpose of promoting international learning and scientific advance, but still more in order to break down the barriers imposed by language between nations and to foster cosmopolitanism. Hegel would have felt none of the interest in the experimental school—the Philanthropinum at Dessau—which Kant and other thinkers of the day exhibited. He was out of sympathy both with the methods it had tried to introduce and the aims it stood for.

In the first place, we shall find that one of the chief merits of a classical language as a means of education appeared to Hegel to lie in the fact of its being unfamiliar, of its having no connection with everyday life, but giving rather the key to a new and far-off world. Its chief value as an aid to self-estrangement would disappear, if once it were substituted for the mother tongue. Then too, he was always opposed to any method that seemed to detract from the dignity and even the solemnity of learning. Latin and Greek appeared to him almost as the signs of an initiation into a higher life, and to have these taught by means of games and playful devices must have struck him as most singularly inappropriate. Nor would Basedow's desire to train up a race of " young cosmopolitans " have appealed to him in the very least. Indeed, cosmopolitanism in any shape, whether intellectual or political, did not really commend itself to Hegel, certainly not as an aim of education. He was a convinced, though not in any sense a narrow, patriot ; and, so far from desiring to supersede the mother tongue, he is in full sympathy with the view which he put forward as being that of his time : " That a nation has no claim to be regarded as cultured which cannot express all the treasures of knowledge in its own tongue and use it with ease for all purposes.   This intimacy with which our own language belongs to us, is lacking to the acquirements which we only possess in a foreign tongue." [1]

Even with regard to philosophy itself, Hegel held strong views as to the importance of presenting it in a national dress and adapting the German language to its requirements.[2]

It was not then from the point of view of utility that Hegel advocated the teaching of the classical languages. All that was necessary for ordinary human life in the way of arts and sciences could be better acquired through the mother tongue.   Hegel is indeed careful to point out how much the position of Latin in education has changed in this respect.   He recalls the position formerly held by the study of Latin, when it counted not merely as one element of learning, but as its essential part, and the only means of higher education offered to those who did not remain satisfied with the general public elementary instruction.[3]   All subjects were supposed to be covered by it, and through its medium even scientific and practical knowledge was to be acquired, with what unsatisfactory results can be imagined.

Hegel saw clearly that the study of science and practical subjects through the classics, meant that these were kept at the level of knowledge attained in classical times, whereas they are in their very nature progressive.

[1] XVI. First address.   [2] Letter to Voss.
[3] XVI. First address.

Moreover, the barrier of a foreign language (important as he shows this to be in another connection) is quite out of place when it is a matter of acquiring facts, and proves an unnecessary hindrance. He puts these views forward in the following way :

" It appears to be a just demand that the culture, art and science of a nation should stand on its own feet. Dare we not have confidence in the culture of the modern world, in our own enlightenment and in the progress of all art and science ? Arts and sciences have passed from the childhood stage they were in at the times of the Greeks and Romans. They have outgrown their old swaddling bands and have become strong enough to stand alone." [1]

As studied in the classics they have only historical value and no utility for the present day, unless indeed as rousing interest and serving as a starting point for further study. He urges further that even such stores of knowledge as we may acquire through another language are not fully our own—" they are separated from us by a barrier which does not allow them to be made truly at home in the mind." [2]

All these false claims for the supremacy of the classics must be set aside : they but obscure the real value of their study and bring it into disrepute.

Hegel admits that, in view of the extremely unsatisfactory results of the type of classical education which was then too commonly met with—a degenerate offspring of the Renascence—he could quite understand even the suggestion that it should be completely

[1] XVI. First address. [2] *Ibid.*

H

abolished. He rejoices, however, in the fact that instead of " this apparently easy way " of dealing with
the difficulty, the Government (through Niethammer's
Normativ) " has satisfied in the really right way the
need of the age by bringing these old elements of culture
into a new relation with the whole ; and thus the essential
value of the older education is as much preserved, as it
is changed and renewed." [1]

He considers that, in truth, the classical languages have
really gained a much surer position and dignity through
the more exact definition of their place in the school
curriculum, and the limitation of the extravagant claims
formerly made on their behalf. The study of the
classics " has lost its exclusiveness and may be regarded
as having overcome the animosity which was roused
by its former arrogance." Through this separation
from other subjects " it has gained its rightful place and
the possibility of developing much more freely."

Let us now turn to the consideration of the positive
claims which he puts forward on behalf of the classical
languages to a definite and even to a first place in the
gymnasium curriculum.

These claims may be conveniently, although at the
risk of some overlapping, considered under the following
heads :

(a) The classics as affording the most suitable mental
food on which to nourish the growing mind at the stage
of secondary school instruction :

    I. Because of the fundamental and unique value of
       the ideas contained in them.

[1] XVI. First address.

II. Because these studies form the necessary basis for later university work.

III. Because in them are found combined, material on which the mind can both be nourished and exercised.

(b) The study of Latin and Greek as the surest means of securing that the step of self-estrangement shall be effectively taken.

(c) The grammars and literatures of the classical languages as offering the best opportunities for developing the power of thought in all its stages.

(d) The function of classical literatures in promoting the growth of certain important aspects of ethical life.

(e) The awakening of the human mind to a true appreciation of the beauty, joy and value of life through a study of the classics.

(a) I. We have already gathered Hegel's general view as to the true function of the secondary school which prepares its pupils for the university. The world of ideas—of thought—is to be unlocked for them, and they must be made at home in this new sphere of experience. But it is essential that it shall be in truth a world rich in living ideas, full of the noblest products of human thought and no arid, dreary intellectual desert to which they are introduced.

"Now in comparison with the literary works belonging to any other time or nation, the classics contain incomparably more of the noblest intellectual and moral nutriment, expressed in the noblest form— golden apples in silver dishes." "There was never found united within the compass of any other civilisation, so much that is excellent, worthy of admiration, original, many-sided and instructive." [1]

The life and ideas of classical times must be fully absorbed and made their own by the pupils. This is absolutely necessary because according to Hegel, intellectual and moral education cannot " be regarded as the steady lengthening of a chain, to whose first links the succeeding ones are added without need for further elaboration of the earlier ones. In education some material and experience is necessary upon which it can work and effect changes." [2]

In the classical literatures, then, are supplied those simple fundamental ideas of life and conduct belonging to the youth of the race, and therefore suited for the study of youth, which form the best possible material for the educator to work upon. He will help the pupils to develop, increase and modify these fundamental ideas ; and gradually through the educational process secure that they shall become effective for present-day life. " It is necessary to win for ourselves the world of antiquity, not only so as to possess it, but still more so as to have something that we can work upon." [3]

Hegel is very emphatic on the point that the material or groundwork for future elaboration must be of the very best. We must " make a beginning with something excellent in itself " ; and, if so, then " the literature of the Greeks in particular, and next that of the Romans, must be and remain the foundation of all higher

---

[1] XVI. First address   [2] *Ibid.*
[3] *Ibid.* The reference here is of course to Goethe's lines :
       "Was du ererbt von deinen Vätern hast
       Erwirb es, um es zu besitzen."

studies." [1]   The order is significant.   If Hegel had had
the disciplinary or utilitarian values in view the order
would surely have been reversed.   As it stands, it seems
clear that what he had in mind was rather the value
for life and conduct.

Greek literature has on the whole a much richer and
more valuable content than is to be found in the Latin
classics, and moreover the Greeks stand for the boyhood
of the race, while the Romans represent a stage of
greater maturity; and boys would at first find more
suitable mental food with the former than with the
latter.   That it was the value for life that he wished to
emphasise, would seem to be borne out by his statement
that an effective study of the classics implies that—" we
must ourselves live with them " (the Greeks and Romans),
" share their pleasures, their ideas, their customs, even
. . . absorb their errors and prejudices." [2]

Thus and thus only could their life be fully realised,
their ideas and thought become in truth the pupils' own.
It is perhaps a little curious that he did not suggest that
the study of the Greek language should precede that of
the Latin.   It may be that he did not feel free to press
this change from the usual order adopted in schools,
but more probably he recognised that as a language
Latin was easier to acquire than Greek.

II. It is clear also that Hegel regarded a study of the
classics as the only sure basis for what he terms the
" learned studies " to be pursued at the university, to
which the gymnasium was the recognised, if not the only
avenue.   In his day of course Philosophy, Law, Theology,

[1] XVI. First address.   [2] *Ibid.*

and Philology would have been the chief subjects to
which his pupils would devote themselves on proceeding
to the university ; and for all these he believed a study
of the classics afforded the best raw material and starting point.   He put this view very definitely before his
pupils and their parents : " The spirit and aim of our
School is preparation for learned pursuits (University
Studies)—a preparation based indeed on the study of the
Greek and Roman classics.   For centuries this has been
the foundation on which all culture has rested, out of
which it has sprung and with which it has remained in
unbroken connection." [1]

Again he urges that, " in the study of the classics,
which is the special object of the school curriculum,
there are found the beginnings and the fundamental
conceptions of all that is worth knowing." [2]

At first sight this insistence on the importance of the
classics as the true basis of culture seems to be somewhat
at variance with his statement, quoted above, that
" the art and science of a nation should stand on its
own feet."   It is necessary to bear in mind, however,
that he was then referring to practical arts and experimental sciences, with regard to which, however true
it may be that they have grown out of earlier efforts,
yet it can hardly be said that it is necessary to success
in them, that they should be studied historically.   It
was quite otherwise, he considered, with those purely
intellectual and moral ideas involved in the university
studies now under discussion.   The complexity of the
ideas and problems presented in them is such that the

[1] XVI. First address.   [2] XVI. Fourth address.

mind needs to be carefully prepared by study of the earlier ideas and simpler problems, before it can be fit to deal successfully with those that are more difficult and complex.

Interested as he undoubtedly was in the attempt to begin the study of philosophy in the school, he yet relied largely on the study of the classics to supply the necessary store of simple, basic ideas on which to work.

III. One further signal advantage Hegel claims for classical studies, is that of economy. Knowledge and power may both be gained at the same time, with one expenditure of effort. No better material for study can be found and no better opportunity for intellectual exercise.

" As the plant, surrounded by light and air, not only exercises its reproductive and other functions, but at the same time absorbs its food, so also must the material upon which the intellect and powers of the mind generally exercise and develop themselves—be in itself a means of nourishment." [1] In the classics the mental food has to be obtained through the medium of unfamiliar languages, the acquirement of which exercises the mind in observing, comparing, generalising, abstracting, judging and reasoning. According to his view, these functions of the mind should always be developed in relation to the best material obtainable ; for the relation of form and matter is so close, that it is extremely undesirable to attempt to separate them.

(b) Hegel's views with regard to the necessity for the step of self-estrangement in the evolution process of every really educated man, have already been considered ; and

[1] XVI. First address.

it only remains for us to note briefly the ways in which a study of the classics might be used to forward this end.

First, as regards subject matter, the classical literatures open up a world remote in time, a world full of men and women, of cities and countries, comedy and tragedy, hopes and fears, which, vivid and clear-cut though they may be, are yet removed from the world of sense and known only in imagination and in thought ; but a world too in which the boy speedily makes himself at home, and from which he can return the richer and the better for his travels.   Then, from the point of view of language, Latin and Greek, being unfamiliar, unconnected with everyday life, emphasise the sense of something foreign and remote, while the time occupied in overcoming the difficulties involved in learning them, seems to mark out the distance traversed.

He also realises better, what from a moral point of view is so important, how far he has travelled from his particular personal life to that manifestation of the universal life which he strives to comprehend in classical literature.

" If we apply this universal necessity (*i.e.* centrifugal force or self-estrangement), under which is included the world of imagination as well as the study of language— to the learning of the latter, then it becomes clear, that the mechanical aspect of such study, is more than a merely necessary evil.   For the mechanical is something foreign to the mind, which however finds interest in it, because thus the crude and indigestible can be assimilated; the mind animates the lifeless, and makes it his own." [1]

[1] XVI. First address.

(c) In the acquirement of the classical languages grammar plays an important part, and Hegel is careful to point out its value in developing thought power at secondary school age. " With the mechanical elements of language learning, the study of grammar is intimately connected. Its worth cannot be too highly estimated, for it serves as the beginning of logical training." " Grammar includes the special products and definitions of reason, and in it also reason first gets practice and skill. The intellectual realities with which grammar first makes us acquainted are easily understood by youth, indeed nothing intellectual is more comprehensible." " The as yet limited powers of youth cannot grasp the riches of the intellectual kingdom in all its variety— but these abstractions (i.e. of grammar) are completely simple. They are comparable to the single letters of the alphabet, and indeed they are the intellectual vowels with which we learn to spell and then to read in the kingdom of thought. Grammar is thus specially adapted for youth at this age, in that it teaches how to distinguish these (simple abstractions) by means of the external characteristics which language usually exhibits." [1] Hegel suggests that youth should be trained so as to distinguish the simple, abstract grammatical ideas by means of their language forms, as easily and as readily as red is distinguished from blue.

Because we are intelligent beings the elements of thought and reason can be, by practice at the right stage, made as directly perceptible to the mind as colours or

[1] XVI. First address.

any aspect of the material world are perceptible to the
sense organs.   If then, these elements or simplest thought
conditions are within our reach, " the first step in education is to become possessed of them, that is to say, to make
them objects of consciousness and to be able to distinguish
them."   Grammar being thus " elementary philosophy "
it should, he thinks, be regarded not only as a means,
but as an end, both in the study of Latin and German.
But Latin grammar has advantages over that of the
mother tongue.

   " The grammatical study of an ancient language has,
however, the advantage of being necessarily a continuous
and uninterrupted activity of the reason, since here
unreflecting habit does not, as in the mother tongue,
produce the correct syntax.   It is needful to have in
view the value of the parts of speech as determined by
reason, and to call to one's aid the rules for their con-
tinuation.   Together with this there also takes place a
continual exercise in bringing the particular under the
general and in defining the general." [1]   Thus the mind
is trained to correct and definite thinking.

   It is also obvious that exercise in observation and
practice of literary form and style would develop facility
in judgment and discrimination.   Hegel seems also
fully to have realised the immense importance, from the
point of view of moral and intellectual training, of the
constant exercise in judgment and reasoning which
could hardly fail to result from the vivid portrayal of
life and conduct, event and consequent, set forth in the
classical literatures.

[1] XVI. First address.

There men and actions could be estimated and judged in an intellectual region, free from all bias of passion, personal prejudice or interest. But this consideration leads on to the next point we have to take into account, and must be more closely examined in that connection.

(d) If " pedagogy is the art of making men moral," [1] it is obvious that Hegel would not have given such prominence to classical studies, had he not believed that they afforded a most important means of moral training. Concrete examples of virtue to be emulated, of vice to be avoided, are simply and clearly set forth in the classics, and unconsciously become for the pupils guides to life and conduct.

But there was more than this implied in his view of morality. The ethical life meant for him far more than simple personal virtues and guiltlessness. It was rather to be thought of as being universal in its nature, and requiring for its realisation the social relations of the family, the community and the state. The truly ethical life is to be lived in the world, not apart from it. " The nature of man is essentially universal, potentially moral ; so it is the essence of education and of thought . . . that the ' I ' should be apprehended as a universal person." [2] This means that the growing mind must be led to reflect upon social relationships as a necessary stage of its training and development. But the boy grows up in a world in which these relationships have become complex and difficult to understand, and it is necessary to find a suitable training ground elsewhere. For this purpose Hegel maintains there is none better

[1] VIII. 218.   [2] VIII. 209.

than the field of classical literature. Family and civic
life are there set forth in such a way as to emphasise
the simple ethical ideas of which they were the expression.   Greek literature in particular affords the best
concrete examples of the State as the realised ethical
idea or ethical spirit. As he tells us, " the classical
period stands in the happy mean between the crude
simplicity of a nation in its ignorant childhood and the
refined intellect and judgment of the civilisation which
has analysed and specialised everything." [1] Everything too is on a much smaller scale—the activities
at work are simpler and more direct, so that we can, as
it were, study universal ethical life in the making, and
by means of concrete examples, at every stage.

It was just this concreteness that Hegel was so anxious
to ensure. It has already been noted that he was a
nationalist rather than a cosmopolitan ; and while he was
very anxious to secure that man shall realise his universality—his true freedom—yet he held it to be no less
important that he shall be able to set limits to himself,
and as member of a definite class, profession, city and
country, help to actualise the ethical life—and to forward in every way its expression in concrete form.
" Man must be accounted a universal being, not because
he is a Jew, Catholic, Protestant, German or Italian, but
because he is a man. This thinking or reflective consciousness is of infinite importance. It is defective only
when it plumes itself upon being cosmopolitan, in
opposition to the concrete life of the citizen." [2] The
claim which Hegel puts forward on behalf of the

[1] XVI. Fourth address.   [2] VIII. 209.

classics in regard to ethical training, is certainly not one to be lightly set aside. Most people would be inclined to agree with him, in thinking that at the age of secondary school instruction it would be difficult, if not impossible, to find any other subject so suitable for the purpose. Even if it be contended that other nations may have had as valuable a historical development, it is at least clear that they do not possess literatures recording this special stage of ethical life and growth,—at least none which can be placed in the same rank.

(e) The last of Hegel's claims on behalf of classical studies, which remains for us to consider, is that which he makes mainly on æsthetic grounds. Life, in order to be complete, must include elements not only of the true and the good, but also of the beautiful. Man must be educated to appreciate beauty and to realise it in his daily life. We know that Hegel himself keenly enjoyed music and other forms of art, but he was particularly alive to the world of beauty which is to be found in literature, and especially in the classical literatures.

He does not say much about other forms of æsthetic training in the school. Probably in his day it was not easy to introduce anything else,—except perhaps music. But he is very emphatic as to the importance of making the boys familiar, at the right age, with the beautiful in language and literature. He constantly refers to the two together—each the necessary counterpart of the other. The original language in which literature appears is always for him the musical element, the fine fragrance, of beautiful thought, without which the ideas themselves lose half their charm and value. Translations may give us the ideas, the thoughts of the author, but the true living beauty can never be rendered thus. He compares them to " artificial roses, which may resemble nature in shape, colour, perhaps even in smell—but the charm, tenderness and delicacy of life is not theirs." [1] In the classical literatures the beauty of thought is bound up with beauty of form, and the pupil must be taught to appreciate both ; the wonder and glory of the world of beauty revealed in classical literature formed the theme of some of Hegel's finest utterances.

No scholar of the Renascence ever gave expression to a more genuine enthusiasm for the literature of the golden age than he does when he tells of " that Paradise of the human mind that in its lovely reality, freedom, depth and brightness comes forth as the bride from her chamber. The first wild glory of the dawn in the east . . . is softened into beauty . . . I believe I do not assert too much, if I say, that whoever lives without knowing the works of the classical writers lives without knowing beauty." And again, when he says that " the completeness and splendour of these masterpieces must be the spiritual bath, the secular baptism, which gives the mind its first and indelible tone and tincture in regard to taste." [2]

Hegel was no pessimist, his outlook on life was rather that of healthy optimism. He desired that boys might be trained to view life sanely and to appreciate the importance of balance and harmony in life. All this, he held, a study of the classics would help them to do, so

[1] XVI. First address.   [2] *Ibid.*

that when they became men they would have the ideal of perfect citizen life before their eyes, and be inspired to lead harmonious lives in the service of the State— while the same study would give them also the key to that " lovely retreat " where they might withdraw for solace and refreshment when weary with professional and other work. Through the magic gate of language this classic land of beauty is entered, and by imagination and thought remains an abiding possession of beauty and enchantment.

It is perhaps unnecessary to add much in regard to the method of teaching the classics which Hegel advocated. From what has already been said, it is obvious that both Greek and Latin were to be studied so thoroughly that their literatures could be read with ease. But to facility in reading, sound grammatical knowledge must be added, and in later school years practice in composition.

There is nothing to indicate that Hegel had any special teaching devices. The pupils must be led to think about both grammar and literature, and no mere rote learning would suffice, but beyond this general requirement, that interest and thought must be roused, he followed recognised methods of instruction.

CHAPTER XII

MORAL EDUCATION AND THE PROPÄDEUTIK

IT has perhaps already been made sufficiently clear that from Hegel's standpoint the whole of the educational process is or should be moral education. For him, no less than for Herbart, morality is the goal of all educational effort. Whereas, however, for Herbart, moral character is that which is formed or built up through instruction and without the assistance of any directing living power within—an edifice designed from without, owing its harmony and utility to the skilful combination and arrangement of the material used in its construction, for Hegel the attainment of morality really implies entering into possession of one's birthright. According to him freedom is the essential characteristic of mind and spirit—implicit in each human being—and the ethical life is the only free life. Moral character is for him, not so much an edifice as a living organism, which unfolds itself according to the inner law of man's being. This unfolding is not merely hastened, it is alone properly secured through education, both instruction and discipline being absolutely necessary. Man becomes moral largely by means of the ideas he assimilates, and his moral life grows and develops when nourished by ideas appropriate to his stage of evolution, which are presented to him through instruction. Yet the mind is always to be regarded as having life in itself, a deeper, truer life even than that of the body; and although needing all possible guidance and nourishment in order that it may develop to best advantage, it exercises a certain selective power, and is never entirely the sport of circumstance.

In moral education therefore, it is all important to secure the active co-operation of the growing self-consciousness. At first of course this will count for little; but gradually, and as it gains in strength, it must be taken more and more into consideration, until at last the moral life is the direct outcome of the life of thought, and man has entered into his true kingdom. He will then appear as a self-governing human being, free because he has identified himself with the universal life of moral thought, of law and order. This is of course the ideal state of things, to which by no means all attain. Hegel is careful to point out that some never realise their freedom, which implies, of course, that they never reach the truly ethical life. He tells us that the criminal, for instance, regards punishment as inflicted by external authority, and does not recognise that it is indeed only the manifestation of his own evil will.[1] He is intellectually deficient, at least to some extent, inasmuch as he does not realise the true relation between cause and effect. This may be the result of some brain defect or weakness, which prevents its proper use as an instrument for thinking, or it may point to some lack or some mistake in education. In any case, man does not attain the

[1] VI. 278.

moral life by chance or by his own unaided efforts. The educator must therefore consider with the utmost care the means which he can successfully employ to secure this desired end.

The means which Hegel considers as chiefly effective are the following : Example ; Moral Atmosphere (including Discipline) ; Indirect Moral Instruction through the Arts and Sciences ; Direct Moral Instruction.

On the first of these he lays great stress, especially with regard to early life. The child at the stage when sense perception is dominant, will of course watch his elders very closely : they are to him indeed the external embodiment of law and authority. He naturally considers that what they do must be right, and imitates them accordingly. " Good example, surrounding them in daily life, is the best training for children." [1] In the family and in the school, the power of example, operating through the child's natural impulse to imitation, is further reinforced by what Hegel terms " moral atmosphere." According to him, it is of the utmost importance that the growing boy shall live in an atmosphere of morality, so that unconsciously the ethical life may become to him his natural element. This atmosphere includes more than example, it implies the introduction of method and order into life.

It is thus closely connected with what is usually termed discipline, which really means securing the proper attitude (whether of mind or body) of the young towards recognised superiority. It is the necessary condition of school instruction, and the foundation

[1] " Urkundon," p. 167.

work in it must be undertaken by the parents
before school age begins, so that by the time the
child enters a secondary school, habitual good behaviour should have been secured. The real meaning
and importance of discipline is to be found in the fact
that it is part of the process of liberation. The un-
disciplined human being is not free, his lower nature
and chance desires rule him, and these are so strong
that he needs all the help which external authority can
give, in order that his life may develop and reach higher
levels of experience. The true significance of obedience
is thus made clear: it is always the recognition of
superiority, or that which is in some way higher and
better; and the controlling of the lower in order to give
prominence to some higher life force. Obedience to
external authority is the first necessary step towards
the attainment of that self-control which is essential
for all intellectual and moral progress. Later on, this
obedience will be gradually transferred (at least if the
work of education has been properly carried out) to the
internal authority of the moral self, the ascendancy of
which implies an ever-increasing degree of freedom. It
is obvious that custom and habit may here prove of the
greatest assistance. Obedience to that which is recognised as superior (parents and teachers, and, later,
rules and accepted customs) must be required as a matter
of course, and so the habit may be formed of regulating
life by higher considerations than those of the natural
impulses and desires. Punishment finds its place here,
as a necessary method of emphasising the results of
yielding to the latter, if they conflict with what is ac-

cepted by common consent as morally or universally good.

Hegel was always a great believer in the value of habit as an aid to intellectual and moral development. The familiar, the customary, the habitual make a strong appeal to children, of whom it is often said that they are by nature conservative. To utilise this tendency, in order to confirm them in right conduct, is clearly the most economical and effective method of procedure; here Hegel was in sympathy with Locke and others who advocate that children should be trained to do right things, without previous conscious reflection upon them.

But Hegel realised too, that there are limits to the value of habit. Even good habits tend to clash with each other, and in any case mere custom can be no sure guide in solving the many difficult problems of conduct which arise in life. Then, as we have already seen, he held that a time comes in the boy's life when the desire for self-estrangement manifests itself. This step implies a breaking away from the familiar and the customary, and although it eventually leads to a new habituation of the mind—to making it at home in a world which at first appears foreign and far off—yet it is clear that from henceforth it is no longer blind habit that will rule. The intellect and the will are gaining freedom, and can in future only be bound by that with which they choose to become identified.

It is especially at this age that Hegel felt the importance of the indirect moral education which results from the study of the arts and sciences, and also of direct moral instruction. We have already seen that he laid great stress on the first of these, especially in connection with classical studies.   Ideals of life and conduct must be presented to the growing mind, and in the classics and literature and history generally, various possibilities are, as it were, presented in sample.

It is clear, however, that he did not intend to limit the moral effect of school work to one kind of study. He made no sharp division between intellectual and moral training ; the ideas and exercises which promote the one have also their value for the other.   Literature and history are perhaps specially rich in ideas which bear directly on human life ; but human life is part of the life of the universe, and nothing can really be regarded as alien to the mind.   Science makes its important contribution of ideas as well as literature, and affords such special training and discipline as cannot be safely neglected.

The moral life, although by its very nature universal, is yet limited in its expression by the personality.   Each one must, at least to some extent, select and determine the kind of life he will lead ; and this choice must necessarily be largely influenced by his school studies and the books he reads.

It is, however, in connection with direct moral instruction, that Hegel makes what is perhaps his most striking contribution to the subject of moral education.   Many have expressed similar views to his with regard to the importance of example, habit, atmosphere and the indirect effect of school studies on the growth of moral character, but few have ventured to deal with the difficult problem of direct moral instruction.   As a rule it is only mentioned, if at all, in connection with religious teaching; and even then it seems to be supposed that its true significance and the proper method of procedure will come by the light of nature. How far this is from being the case, perhaps only those know who have really tried to give this kind of teaching, although its failure to produce the desired results on life and conduct is perhaps sufficiently obvious. The value of Hegel's contribution is greatly enhanced by the fact that it is not only a theoretical position which he gives us, but the result of several years of actual teaching experience.

He himself gave all the religious, moral and philosophical instruction for about eight years to the boys in the gymnasial classes of his school (*i.e.* from about fourteen to eighteen years of age) and he was of course, as headmaster, responsible for the supervision of the rest of instruction given in the school.

We gather from what Hegel says, that the problem of moral instruction was being widely discussed at that time, and perhaps not always in the wisest way. Both he and Niethammer realised the extreme importance of the whole question, and while others were only talking about it, they directed their energies towards formulating and getting into working order a practical scheme of study, which should combine, in one course, moral, religious and philosophic instruction and be especially adapted to meet the needs of secondary schools. It was in the first instance drawn up in outline by Niethammer, but was modified, interpreted and given its detailed content by Hegel and, as adopted finally in his school, was practically his own.

This scheme was the subject of much correspondence between the two friends, and it is clear from Hegel's letters how keenly he was interested in making this part of the school instruction really successful. In spite of occasional doubts, and of certain difficulties which could only, after all, be expected in connection with such pioneer work, it appears quite clear that on the whole he was satisfied with the results of his experiments in teaching. Even his doubts and difficulties seem to be confined to the more purely philosophic part of the course, and were perhaps chiefly connected with the question of the proper place, if any, for logic in the school curriculum. The scheme, as finally elaborated by Hegel, is known as the Propädeutik, and is so arranged as to serve not only as an introduction to the more serious study of philosophy which might be pursued later at the university, but also as a means of providing suitable moral instruction and securing proper reflection upon religious matters. For Hegel there was no barrier between philosophy and religion; each was necessary to the other, and morality was bound up with both. It is important to bear in mind his view of the essential unity of the intellectual and spiritual side of man. These are no two worlds to be kept distinct; it is, on the contrary, not only possible but necessary to develop and keep them together in the closest union. The spiritual world is truly attained through thought, and even religious emotion should be emotion at the thought level and not the blind feeling characteristic of the natural man. We must now turn to the content of the Propädeutik in order to consider in more detail the plan of instruction carried out by Hegel. His biographer, Rosenkranz, who discovered the manuscript (in the autumn of 1838) amongst some papers that had been overlooked, was fortunately able to include it in the first collected edition of his works published in 1840. He tells us of the way in which Hegel had evidently corrected and recorrected, altered and improved the original draft, so that the manuscript presented a patchwork appearance in red and black ink and pencil.

Hegel clearly took the work very seriously, prepared each lesson with great care, and, not content merely to repeat his courses year by year, revised and altered them as seemed necessary.

We have already referred to his method of teaching, so it is only necessary to recall that the boys were always expected to take part in the lesson, to recapitulate what they had learned in the last, to discuss points as they arose and to ask questions when anything was not clear to them. He gave them notes on each lesson and required written work to be done at home.

Four hours per week were given in each of the gymnasial classes, and the courses were arranged as follows :

1st *Course.* Lower Gymnasial Class (age about 14 to 15). Theory of Right, Duty and Religion:

I. Ideas of Right and Justice.
II. Ideas of Duty or Morality.
III. Religious Ideas.

2nd Course.   Middle Gymnasial Class (age 15 to 17 or 18).
   Psychology and Logic :
      A. Psychology :
         I. Consciousness in general.
         II. Self-consciousness.
         III. Reason or Human Understanding.
      B. Logic :
         I. Being.
         II. Existence, The Kantian Antinomies.
         III. Conception.

3rd Course.   Upper Gymnasial Class (age 17 to 20).
   Theory of the Concept and Philosophical Encyclopædia :
      A. Theory of the Concept :
         I. The Concept.
         II. Realisation of the Concept.
         III. Theory of Ideas.
      B. Philosophical Encyclopædia :
         I. Logic.
         II. Natural Science.
         III. Mental Science.

These courses differ somewhat from those suggested
by Niethammer, chiefly, however, as regards the order
of the subjects.   For instance, in the lower class Logic
was to have been taken and religious ideas to be treated
before those relating to rights and duties.   Hegel appears
to have tried this plan the first year, but found the order
unsatisfactory and Logic an unsuitable subject for boys
at that age.   He writes thus to Niethammer : " I have
always found with this class a greater interest in practical

than in the more theoretical ideas which I have had to present, and I felt this difference in interest still more when I at first tried to begin with the fundamental ideas of Logic. Since then I have not repeated the attempt." " Logic is an abstract study and has only a theoretical content and no immediate reality for the mind." " The logical distinctions of Universal and Particular, etc., are to the mind, which is not yet at home in thinking, shadows as opposed to reality." [1]

He finally decided to alter the order of subjects, to postpone Logic until the middle class and to treat of Rights and Duties before Religion in the lower class. He carefully explains to Niethammer that his reason for beginning with Rights and Duties is that the ideas involved are not only simpler and more easily understood than those connected with religion, but that they really form the necessary basis for the study of the latter. It must, of course, be remembered, that Hegel was not advocating the entire postponement of religious instruction. The boys would have had it regularly up to the age of fourteen; but in this year, when they were to be brought for the first time to reflect upon these ideas and make them consciously their own, he held that the growing mind must learn to understand the nature of rights before it can realise duties, and that only then will it be in a position to grasp the more abstract religious ideas. Arranged thus, Hegel seems to have felt satisfied that this was a suitable course, and he refers to it thus : " The concepts of this instruction are simple and have at the same time a content that makes them quite suitable for

[1] Letter to Niethammer, 23rd October 1812,

the age of these pupils. The content is supported by their natural feeling; it has a reality for their hearts." "Freedom, right, possession, etc., are practical ideas with which we daily have to do, which make an immediate appeal to the mind and have also a recognised existence and worth." [1]

With regard to the points actually dealt with by Hegel in his teaching, we must confine ourselves to the briefest statement. "Right and Justice" he considered in connection both with the individual and the community; the freedom of the individual and its possible limitations, work, property, contract, etc.; the rights of the community both as family and as state, the meaning of law and government; and the functions and forms of the latter. "Duties and Morality" were treated in relation to : (1) The Self ; (2) The Family ; (3) The State ; (4) Mankind generally. In the section devoted to the subject of "Religion" such ideas as conscience, faith ; the meaning of religion ; God and His attributes ; the meaning of sin, were dealt with. According to the "Normativ" the subject matter for the second course was to include (a) Cosmology, Natural Theology in connection with Kant's Critique; (b) Psychology. This arrangement was in practice considerably modified by Hegel. Logic was introduced and practically took the place of (a) ; (b) was retained, but realising the impossibility of doing jutice to both Logic and Psychology if taken together in one year, he was accustomed to take them alternately. As boys were expected to spend at least two years in this class, they were thus able to study both. Of the four

[1] Letter to Niethammer.

hours weekly allotted for this course, Hegel found it best after a time to reserve one hour for more definite religious instruction. At first sight it is perhaps not easy to see that there is any connection between moral education and the study of Logic and Psychology, but we must remember that both of these, as taught by him, were far removed from the formal, classificatory kinds, often considered as the only possible for beginners. His Logic course included a consideration of the wider conditions of thought, existence, space, time, etc.; the thought-life as a whole as well as its forms. In Psychology too he dealt rather with the gradual development of consciousness, the way in which mind works its way towards freedom, and the importance of these processes for the individual and for the race, than with detailed analysis of mental phenomena. In this way these subjects became truly moral instruction and of the utmost value for life and conduct.

In the third course Hegel adhered pretty closely to Niethammer's suggestion of a philosophic encyclopædia. He first deals with the fundamental logical ideas underlying all knowledge, and then proceeds to apply these to a consideration of the various sciences. The sciences of Nature—viz., Mathematics, Physics, Chemistry, Geology, Physiology, etc., are grouped together and dealt with in turn. Then comes the Philosophy of Mind, which he treats of under three divisions—viz.: (1) The concept of mind and its psychology. Here he gives some classification of mental phenomena. (2) The realisation of mind (through moral life and conduct and in the life of the State). (3) The perfection of mind or spirit in Art, Religion, and Science.

It would take too long to enter into more detail as to his treatment of this most interesting and suggestive part of the scheme to which he devotes about eighty pages of the Propädeutik ; but it is obvious that no boy who had followed this course, could leave school without some insight into the value and meaning of life and some sense of human responsibility and destiny. In connection with this course of instruction, we must not forget that it was also intended to serve the purpose of an introduction to the study of philosophy at the university. Philosophy has always suffered from the fact that to most of the students entering a university it is an unknown region of study. Theological students, and to a limited extent those who look forward to teaching, are, as a rule, the only ones who venture to explore this subject, which yet has such a close and important bearing on life and also on other subjects of study. Niethammer was very anxious to secure that philosophy should be properly and systematically taught in the gymnasium, but his enthusiasm led him too far, and here Hegel exercised a valuable restraining influence. The latter insisted that it was not so much the formal, systematic teaching of philosophy that was needed, as the inculcation of philosophical ideas in their direct connection with practical life and school studies. In one of his letters he even expresses the view that possibly a thorough study of classical literature would give all that was necessary. It seems clear, however, that, with certain modifications, he came not only to accept the view that the combined course of religious, moral and philosophic instruction proposed by Niethammer was good in itself, but that it also served as an excellent introduction to the study of philosophy. In writing to Niethammer he says : " If the question is asked, whether this subject matter is suitable as an introduction to the study of Philosphy, I can only answer in the affirmative." At the same time, as we have already seen, he insisted on some alterations in the original plan. Logic was postponed from the first to the second course ; the study of Kant is reduced to some consideration of the antinomies ; classificatory treatment both in Logic and Psychology is either avoided or brought in as late as possible, and finally he resisted all attempts to induce him to include History of Philosophy in the school curriculum. At school age any endeavour to sum up and compare different systems of philosophy could lead to nothing more than the use of empty words, and this he always set his face against. The practice of including philosophy in the school curriculum became widespread in Germany. It was of course not entirely a new idea. Some philosophy—mainly Logic—had indeed been included in the curriculum of the schools of the Middle Ages, but it had dropped out and probably had never been made much of. From the time of Hegel's work at Nürnberg until about the middle of the nineteenth century, however, the subject had great vogue. Rosenkranz, writing in 1840, mentions it as being still a branch of ordinary school study. Since then, however, it has tended to be generally crowded out, together with other humanistic studies, in order to make room for subjects having more scientific and commercial value. Professor Paulsen, in his recent book on " German

Education," deplores this, and writes very warmly in favour of its reintroduction in the interests of life and thought—of science itself and still more of religion.

If we now endeavour to sum up Hegel's views in regard to moral education, we shall find that he regarded the problem as presenting different aspects at various stages of life.

In early life, and of course, therefore, mainly in the home, discipline and training in obedience and moral habits counts for most, and had he referred explicitly to elementary schools, he would no doubt have shown that the same would hold good to a large extent there. The force of example means a great deal at this stage, especially if we extend the term slightly to include example, as given, not only by living people, but as set forth in stories and biography. The value of indirect and direct moral instruction seemed to him of special importance at secondary school age, when habits of good behaviour have been established and the mind is thus left free and better able to take in higher ideas and to learn to reflect upon them. He regards it as a very serious matter if parents have neglected their duty in regard to early training, and holds that a school is justified in expelling a boy who has not been taught to behave. A certain amount of civilisation is a necessary condition of higher moral and intellectual education, and a secondary school must require it. A third rather difficult stage occurs towards the end of school life, when the boy begins to think himself a man and is no longer quite content with the quiet round of school

duties and interests. At this point Hegel considers
that the active co-operation of parents and teachers is
absolutely necessary if this period is to be safely traversed.
He refers to the matter several times in his school
addresses, and always tries to show how important it is
to prevent too early participation in grown-up life and
its distractions. Both parents and school must make
earnest efforts to keep the boys steadily at work, and he
urges, for instance, that parents are responsible for
making quiet study at home possible. Strict discipline
must be enforced both in and out of school, and the
parents should inform the masters of any roughness or
unruliness which they have noticed or heard of, so that
the school influence may be used to check it.

It seems almost as if Hegel regarded the last year or
so at school as the most critical time of all. This period
had, of course, for him a special significance as marking,
in most cases, the time of the return journey, when the
youth—long self-estranged and lost in the new intellectual
world he has been exploring—enters into possession of
himself, feels his own power and pulls himself together
before embarking on his life career. The feeling of
approaching maturity and the realisation of his own
capacity for work give him a certain self-confidence
and impatience of control, which renders him difficult to
deal with. Here then is the time for testing the value
of the education he has received ; for, however carefully
arrangements may be made, distractions guarded
against and wrong-doing punished (and all this is due
to the pupil as support to his own efforts), yet the real
guiding force of his life must now be looked for in the

ideas he has assimilated and in the ideals of conduct which he has formed.

At the present moment, when the whole question of moral education is so much to the fore, the value of direct moral instruction so keenly debated, it is of peculiar interest to find that, nearly one hundred years ago, Hegel felt able to state his full belief in the possibility and desirability of both. In connection with the latter, a careful study of the Propädeutik would amply repay any teacher who wishes to give moral instruction in a secondary school, in spite of the extreme compression of its paragraphs and sad lack of explanatory detail.

CHAPTER XIII

HEGEL AND FROEBEL

IT has been sometimes stated by Froebelian enthusiasts that Froebel was the real exponent of Hegelian philosophy in the schoolroom, and that it is to him we must look for the practical outcome of this philosophy in education. The emphasis laid by Froebel upon the leading Hegelian ideas of Unity of Life and its Spiritual Meaning, Development, Reconciliation of Opposites, etc., gives considerable colour to this view, and were we to confine ourselves to these more general statements regarding life and evolution put forward by Hegel and Froebel, it would be hard to find any substantial difference of view between them. It is rather when we turn to their practical work and their written statements concerning educational method that doubts begin to assail us, and the problem is now to find what are points of real agreement, points of difference being so much more apparent.

On the one hand, Hegel is found urging that it is the function of education to assist man to break away from his natural self, from the life which he shares with the world of nature, so that he may attain intellectual and spiritual life—which life is universal. To this end the teacher should not study or follow the individual child, and attempt to adapt his teaching to the demands of the natural human being, but should rather seek to take him out of himself and help him to become self-estranged. This is the true line of human development, that he may learn to identify himself with a higher mental and moral self, a new birth within, only to be attained as a result of obedience, self-abnegation and the discipline of self-estrangement.

As the natural self is drawn towards things of sense and is strengthened by contact with them, Hegel suggests, as we have already seen, that it may even be necessary to become " blind and deaf " to the world of sense, in order that the inner and real life of the mind may develop undisturbed. We find him, therefore, maintaining the superiority of language, literature, history and philosophy, for purposes of instruction, over those subjects which make a more direct appeal to the senses, such as observational science, technical work, etc. He goes so far as to claim for Latin and Greek a peculiar value in this respect, in that they, being dead languages, impose an effectual barrier between the natural self in its everyday surroundings and the developing mind; the truly spiritual self finding its food in a realm of ideas realised concretely in classic times, where, undisturbed by distractions of sense, universal moral and intellectual truths become part of its life.

On the other hand, we find Froebel maintaining that the function of education is to promote the harmonious development of the child, which is indeed the law of nature, but may be helped or hindered by adult human beings. It is, according to him, the teacher's duty to study the individual child, to provide appropriate food for all sides of his nature, to ward off evil influences, but yet in the main to assume rather an attitude of following than of leading.   Although he seems quite to recognise the importance of ultimately attaining full mental and moral life, the way thereto lies for him through things of sense.   Even the most abstract studies —*e.g.* mathematics—have their roots in sense experience.   Hence his insistence on the importance of the training of the senses, in order that this necessary foundation shall be secured.

As a basis for the study of mathematics, for instance, the child must be given ample opportunity to exercise his observational powers upon the geometrical and numerical properties of solids before he can be expected to grapple with geometrical and arithmetical problems stated only in words or symbols.

This gives us the inner meaning of his series of " gifts," the very name of which suggests the idea of something given to the child for his own, and upon which he can exercise his growing powers.   These " gifts " are intended to be presented to the child one by one, beginning with the first—the ball or sphere (the simplest solid form, with only a single surface), proceeding through the cylinder (the connecting link between the sphere and the cube) to the cube—in the second gift, simple and indivisible, and then (in the third, fourth, fifth and sixth), increasingly complex (composed of smaller cubes or other subdivisions) and divisible.   From three-dimensional solids the transition is made, through gifts of tablets (*i.e.* cardboard shapes of different surfaces), sticks and wires (used for outlining figures on the flat and intended to prepare for ideas of line), peas, beads, etc. (to prepare for the idea of a point), to representation of solids in drawing and painting, and therefore in two dimensions only. This stage again affords a starting point for the development of abstract ideas of number and geometric form, and so, by degrees, the child climbs slowly up to the world of mathematical ideas.

It is, according to Froebel, to the child's own activity, expressing itself and gradually growing in power through exercise upon material (physical, mental and moral) that we must look for progress in development. The inner must be made outer, the outer inner. All experience necessary for this development can easily be brought within the child's reach. There is no need to learn dead languages in order to reach a world of appropriate ideas.

Accordingly we find Froebel emphasising the importance of nature study, science and geography, beginning with home environment ; of history and literature, beginning with the child's own daily experiences, recounted orally or in writing, and similar ones as given in books ; of moral and social relations, first realised through family and school life.

Another very striking difference between the two is to be found in the different views each held with regard to play. Hegel wishes the child to learn the seriousness of work as opposed to play, and is emphatically against any attempt to combine the two, or rather to secure work in the form of play. Froebel, on the contrary, regards play seriously as a child's attempt to understand life through a species of dramatic representation, and holds that this natural expression of activity on his part is a guide to the teacher in respect of method. Hence the prominent place given to games in the Kindergarten system.

Many of these apparently wide divergences in method and practice tend, however, to become far less acute, and even in some cases to disappear upon closer examination of the sense in which each makes use of a given term ; but these different uses of the term are of course misleading when any comparison is instituted. The use of the word " nature " affords an illustration. By this term Hegel indicates the antithesis of spirit and limits its use practically to the world of sense experience, whereas with Froebel it is given a much wider significance, and is indeed made to cover all the phenomena of the spontaneously unfolding life of the individual mind.

Then with regard to the meaning of development or evolution : according to Hegel, human development demands a breaking with nature, even if ultimate reconciliation be also implied ; whereas for Froebel human development towards the spiritual is truly a law of nature, and the usual order of development would be harmonious evolution with no break or jar.

Hegel's insistence on the necessity for this break appears, however, to be chiefly in regard to the comparatively few human beings capable of higher development and who approximate more nearly to ideal humanity than the great mass of mankind. The few references he makes to popular elementary education (although it is quite clear that he fully believed it was the duty of the State to provide such, and indeed held strongly that for all classes of society the material of instruction should nourish moral and intellectual life) do not emphasise this point ; and it may be that he regarded it as true that the bulk of the people had hardly reached that level in evolution which demanded this process of self-estrangement.   But we must not forget that this break would not in any case, be likely to occur early in the child's life.   Now Hegel had mainly (if we leave out of account his experience as tutor) to do with boys from fourteen to eighteen, just the period at which wider ideas and interests become real to ordinary youth.   He would naturally concentrate his interest on this period of development and consider school organisation and curriculum with special reference to those at this stage.

Froebel, however, may be said to have been chiefly, though of course not exclusively, interested in the education of young children.   Few have had so deep an insight into their nature, and although he had experience in teaching pupils of all ages, yet it was to the little ones that his thoughts most naturally turned and about them that his most striking pedagogical utterances were made.

It is clear, therefore, that Hegel and Froebel were mainly considering two different stages in human development.

Speaking generally, we may say that in the development of the human being the early years are those in which the general consciousness of external nature is shared— the child is nearer to the life of plants and animals— and that the important thing in education at this stage is for the child to feel that unity of life and share it to the full.[1]

Froebel, having mainly in mind this early stage of development, would be led to emphasise a harmonious unfolding of natural powers, to urge the importance of helping the child to seek for unity amid diversity, to correlate *all* knowledge and to realise his oneness with his environment.

Hegel, in considering a later stage—that roughly covered by secondary school instruction—the stage in which the human being should attain real self-conscious life and freedom, with all that these imply—would therefore naturally concentrate his attention on the problems of development connected with that period, which would include specially the question of how this true life and freedom were to be secured, how far it is necessary to die in order to live, to lose in order to find.

It is not without interest to note that Hegel seems to make a distinction between the sexes in respect of the process of development. He seems to indicate that a woman's course of development is much more harmonious than a man's, and that the break with nature is often hardly perceptible. Still, he frankly admits that he is not clear as to the mode of education suited to women.

Now Froebel boldly faced the question of the education of women, as well as of men. This was of course

---

[1] It is clear from a remarkable passage (vii. p. 90) that Hegel fully realised that the human being had to pass through such a series of stages, and he describes them in language that might have been Froebel's own.

partly because as regards young children there can be no
serious question of difference of sex ; but Froebel further
desired higher education for girls because he regarded
them as future mothers and teachers. If, therefore,
there is any real force in Hegel's view that there is a
difference in the process of development as between men
and women, the fact that he had to deal almost exclusively with boys, while Froebel had much, and towards
the end of his life, perhaps most, to do with the education
of girls (chiefly of course in preparing them for kindergarten teaching), may help to account for their difference
of view.

Further, we must not forget that both were in complete
agreement on one point in connection with evolution—
namely, that the higher explains the lower, that spirit is
implicit in plants and animals and becomes explicit in
man. It is not the plants and animals that determine
the moral and intellectual life of human beings, but human
life, as spiritual, explains and justifies lower forms.

We might bring their general views on this subject
into relation by saying that while both Hegel and Froebel
were in agreement that the methods of all true progress
in knowledge, morals and life generally, is by a process
of reconciliation of opposites, Hegel tended to emphasise
the antagonism first, while Froebel laid chief stress upon
the reconciliation. They both saw the same truth from
different points of view. Hegel's intellect was logical
and scientific ; Froebel's was more intuitional. The
logical mind, in order to apprehend a truth fully, must
first be quite clear about the discrete points involved
before proceeding to a synthesis, whereas an intuitional

mind must grasp the whole, however vaguely, before
the part can be apprehended and properly dealt with.

It is possible that much of the difference between these
two in respect of curriculum, discipline, etc., may be
explained away on similar lines. While Hegel had
constantly before his eyes the needs of secondary
schools for boys intending to proceed to the universities,
Froebel was almost entirely preoccupied with schemes
for popular education of both sexes. Then, as before
noted, they constantly used the same term in entirely
different meanings. We have already considered this
in reference to the term nature, but it may be desirable to add something more on the different uses they
make of the word " play."

Hegel clearly means by play, something opposed to
work, mere relaxation, having no doubt its place and
value in life, but needing to be sharply distinguished
from all that is serious and purposive therein. That use
of the term is of course justified by common usage.
Froebel, however, saw that there were included under
this term two different things which it was important
to distinguish. Children at play not only "let off
steam," as it were, obeying the impulses of nature in
movement, or abandoning themselves to the excitement
and enjoyment of such without any end in view; they
also *play games*, and in perhaps the majority of these—all
indeed that are worthy of the name—we find a definite
idea or ideas worked out and made real to consciousness
by this means. Now Froebel observed that the child's
attitude towards this sort of play was wholly different
from that exhibited towards the first kind. In such

games, for instance, as "keeping shop," "fox and geese," children are entirely serious in intention; and any one of their number who fails to be is taken to task by the others. Of course they will laugh and enjoy themselves too, but what is meant is that they are really intent on working out the main idea of the game.

As said above, it would seem as if children needed thus to objectify life in its different phases and that their love of games is really largely, although of course unconsciously, prompted by their desire to understand life in all its bewildering variety. They want to know by experience what it means to be a shopkeeper, soldier, sailor, teacher, explorer, even bird, beast or plant, and so they take these rôles in turn. The form of this kind of play naturally varies with different stages of development and is partly also determined by environment.

Froebel adopted the " game " as part of his educational method, not merely to make things easy for children, or to beguile them unknowingly into the paths of knowledge, but because he regarded this kind of play as a natural instrument of instruction suited to early childhood; and, so long as this method is not prolonged unduly to an age when other methods are more appropriate, he had no fear that anything but good would result.

In spite of all differences, however, Hegel and Froebel explain and supplement each other. It is possible that they never met and if they had that neither would have really appreciated the other; and yet they both were aiming at doing much the same thing for the world. Both aimed at giving man to himself, so that he might

attain true freedom by realising his oneness with the
universe. But one was ever striving to do this by giving
an intellectual interpretation of the universe, man and
life, while the other sought rather to give a practical
interpretation and to make everyday life experience
the means of enfranchisement. Each is strong where
the other is comparatively weak. Hegel has given to
the world one of the finest philosophies of life, and makes
us realise more clearly than anyone the place and theoretical value of education, its relation not only to the
individual and the community, but also to the evolution
of humanity. Froebel, on the contrary, tends to be
nebulous and unsatisfactory when dealing with pure
theory. He gives the impression of one who is struggling
to express truths that he feels deeply but cannot see
quite clearly. He seems at times to be carried away by
strong ideas over which he has not sufficient mastery, and
it is not easy to reduce his theory to a coherent whole.

If, however, we compare the two men as teachers,
the positions are to a large extent reversed. There is a
certain hard intellectuality about Hegel that must have
made it very difficult for him to get into any real touch
with very immature minds, although with older boys he
seems to have succeeded well. We feel sure that he gave
school instruction clearly and conscientiously, and the
very effort to adapt himself to undeveloped minds must
have reacted advantageously, as he indeed himself
recognises, upon his own thought. But the impression
remains that he was not a born teacher, that educational
work was rather an incident than the all-absorbing
interest of his life.

Far otherwise do we find it with Froebel.   From the moment when he found himself for the first time before a class in school at Frankfurt (which experience he describes as being that of a fish finding itself for the first time in water), until the end of his life, teaching was for him the natural element of his life.   It is difficult to think of him in any other capacity than that of teacher ; and his profession meant for him the joy of life, nay, life itself.   With a sure touch he could enter into relation with immature minds and stimulate their growth. When in contact with little ones he became as a child, able to think and feel and act as one ; and therefore his rallying call to all intending teachers was ever : " Come let us live with our children."

One was the great philosopher, who yet did valuable work for school education generally.   The other was the great teacher and trainer of teachers, who devoted his life to the service of children.

It is unnecessary to push the comparison between the two men further.   We have said enough to show that they were widely different in temperament, life and action, and yet that again and again they come into close relation by reason of their most fundamental views on education.   Perhaps indeed the real interest to be found in any study of their relations is in the effort to effect the reconciliation of apparently opposite personalities.

APPENDIX

EXTRACTS FROM HEGEL'S "SCHOOL ADDRESSES" AND NIETHAMMER'S "NORMATIV"

I. Classical Studies

(Extract from First Address)

THE spirit and aim of our institution is preparation for learned pursuits (University Studies)—a preparation based definitely on the study of the Greek and Roman classics.

For centuries this has been the foundation on which all culture has rested—out of which it has sprung and with which it has remained in unbroken connection.

As natural organisms, plants and animals, can, to some extent, set themselves in opposition to the action of gravity, but yet cannot altogether escape from that necessary element of their existence—so all art and learning have grown out of classical soil, and although they have also become independent, yet have they not freed themselves from the memory of that older culture.

As Antæus renewed his strength by contact with his mother earth, so each new departure and development of knowledge and culture has raised itself to the light of day through a return to antiquity.

And indeed if we admit that it is all important to make a beginning with something excellent in itself, then the literature of the Greeks in particular, and next that of the Romans, must be and remain the foundation of all higher studies.

The perfection and grandeur of these masterpieces must be the intellectual bath, the secular baptism, which gives the mind its first and indelible tone and tincture in respect of good taste and knowledge.

For this initiation a general, superficial acquaintance with the classics is not sufficient. We must ourselves live with them (the Greeks and Romans), share their pleasures, their ideas, their customs, even, if one will, absorb their errors and prejudices, and so become perfectly at home in this, the most beautiful world that has ever existed.

If the first Paradise was the Paradise of human *nature*, this is the second, the higher Paradise of the human *mind*—that in its lovely reality, freedom, depth and brightness, comes forth as the bride from her chamber. The first wild glory of its dawn in the east is restrained by the dignity of form and softened into beauty ; its depth shows itself no longer in confusion, obscurity or arrogance, but lies open and clear before us.   Its brightness is not that of childish play, but covers a hidden sadness ; it knows the hardness of fate, but is not driven thereby from freedom and moderation.

I believe I do not assert too much in saying that, whoever lives without knowledge of the classics lives without knowing beauty.

While we make ourselves at home in such an atmosphere, the result is not merely that all powers of the mind are excited, developed and exercised, but also that we find a supply of unique material with which we enrich our inner life and raise it to a higher level.

It has been said that intellectual activity can be exercised on any kind of material, and that useful knowledge and the objects of sense perception form the most suitable material for instruction, these being best adapted for the age of youth or childhood, because they belong to the circle of experience and mode of representation already proper to it.

Even if it were possible (which is doubtful) to regard the form in which matter appears—the exercise itself—as separable from and indifferent to the objective circle of experience in which it occurs, yet our concern is not merely with exercise.

As the plant, surrounded by light and air, not only exercises its reproductive and other functions, but at the same time absorbs its food, so also must the material —upon which the intellect and the powers of the mind generally exercise and develop themselves—be in itself a means of nourishment. It is not that so-called useful knowledge, that material of sense experience as it comes directly under the child's observation, but the spiritual content—which has value and interest in itself—that alone really strengthens the mind and produces that independent attitude, that true inner power which is the mother of understanding, self-command, discretion, presence of mind and mental alertness.

The mind of one thus nurtured manifests, on attaining maturity, a central core of independent worth, of purposive ends which form the first foundation of all after usefulness in life, and which it is important to cultivate in the mind of those belonging to all ranks of society.

Have we not actually seen in recent times, states which neglected and despised any attempts to secure and develop in the minds of their subjects any such inner characteristics, confining their attention merely to useful subjects (those which concern mind and character being only regarded as formal training—a means to an end) standing helpless in danger, and overthrown in the midst of their many useful devices?

Now in comparison with the literary works belonging to any other time or nation the classics contain incomparably more of the noblest intellectual and moral nutriment, expressed in the noblest form—golden apples in silver dishes.

I need only recall the sublimity of their sentiments, their elevated virtue and patriotism free from all moral ambiguity—the lofty nature of their deeds and characters, the variety of their destinies, their customs and systems of government—to substantiate the assertion that there was never found united within the compass of any other civilisation so much that is excellent, worthy of admiration, original, many-sided and instructive.

This wealth is, however, bound up with language, and only through its medium do we reach its full and proper significance. Translations give us, to some extent, the meaning, but not the form, not its inner ethereal soul. They are like artificial roses which may resemble nature in shape, colour, perhaps even in smell

—but the charm, tenderness and delicacy of life is not theirs.

Language is the musical element, the element of intimacy, which disappears in translation—the fine fragrance by means of which the soul sympathy may be enjoyed, but without which a classic work only tastes like " Rhine wine which has lost its flavour."

This consideration lays on us the apparently hard necessity of studying the classical languages thoroughly, and of making ourselves sufficiently conversant with their literatures to be able to enjoy to the fullest extent all their many-sided and peculiar treasure. If we are inclined to complain of the trouble that this involves, and to fear or regret that the acquirement of other subjects and accomplishments must be neglected, then we should blame fate, that has not allotted to us such a range of classical works in our own language as would have rendered unnecessary the troublesome journey back to antiquity, and have granted us compensation for the loss involved.

II. Discipline

(*Extract from Second Address*)

The question of discipline is an important matter, in relation to which the school stands in necessary connection with home life. I distinguish here between moral training and discipline on the one hand and moral education on the other. The former cannot be the aim of an educational institution, its duty is rather the cultivation of character and the formation of moral habits, and even this not to the fullest possible extent. It is not for the school to begin the moral training of its pupils, it can claim that this be presupposed. We have to require that the children come into our school already trained and disciplined.

According to the spirit and the custom of our time, the direct discipline of the young is not, as among the Spartans, a public matter, an arrangement of the State, but the business and duty of parents. Except in the case of orphanages and boarding schools—those institutions which undertake to care for all sides of the pupils' lives— schools (at least secondary schools) are to be regarded mainly as places of instruction and not directly of training and discipline. This is partly so because the opportunity of giving the first elements of education, whether those of knowledge or of morality—does not fall to their share. From those who attend our school we expect quiet behaviour, the habit of continuous attention, respect and obedience to the teachers and proper and seemly conduct both towards these and towards their fellow-pupils. With children in whom home training has not produced these requirements, the school must attempt to do what it can towards effecting this discipline, by curbing roughness, checking desire for distraction and by in- culcating feelings of respect and of obedience towards teachers and parents, which the latter have found them- selves unable to secure in the home.

Certainly, in the case of most of our pupils, we have found those qualities which are the fruits of careful home training, or even more of a good home example, and with regard to the few exceptions, have been able to note the satisfactory effect of school discipline. At the same time it is necessary to remember that, since it is the essential characteristic of a secondary school that it aims at something more and begins at a higher stage than an ordinary elementary school, any attempt to undertake this early discipline, where it has been previously neglected, can only be regarded as an experiment. If in such neglected cases improvement does not soon begin to show itself, and roughness, disobedience and disorder to disappear, the boys must be sent back to their parents, who may now at length feel obliged to fulfil their duties. Such pupils must be removed from a school where the instruction given is of a kind which cannot become effective on an uncivilised basis.

But though the school presupposes early moral discipline, it yet regards moral education or culture as being in immediate connection with its chief business of instruction both indirectly and directly. We are indeed accustomed to the idea, which has come down to us from the past, of separating head and heart, thinking and feeling, or whatever else this distinction may be termed; of considering them almost as two kinds of existence, independent of and indifferent to each other. According to this view, the influence of instruction on character appears to be remote or casual. But the mind of man is a true unity, and does not include within itself two such totally different natures. Any one-sidedness which is possible to the mind can only concern individual, subordinate powers far removed from the root of its being. Differences and distinctions meet face to face and find themselves at one in the inmost self. There can be no sharp division or cleavage in the mind itself.

General education is bound up most closely with moral education, for we must not limit this latter to a few principles and maxims, to the encouragement of general honesty, kindliness and feeling of honour.

We must go further and hold it as the truth that only the really educated man can be the morally cultivated man.

III. The Training Value of Military Exercises

(*Extract from Second Address*)

During this year (1810) military exercises have formed part of the work of the pupils in the highest class of the school. Such training is of very great importance in education. It implies learning to understand quickly, to have presence of mind, to carry out a command on the spot without previous reflection, and it is the best cure for that state of indolence and distraction of mind which involves waste of time before what is heard is understood, and still more before it results in action. Too often this implies also that the meaning is only half grasped and consequently only half carried out.

This opportunity for taking up a new subject has also demonstrated that if the young are already trained intellectually and have developed some power of attention, they are in a position to acquire with ease anything they desire to learn, to familiarise themselves with it quickly and to make rapid progress.

From another point of view, also, the introduction of
such exercises into the school curriculum appears to be
very advantageous. We are too much accustomed to
regard each particular art and science as something
special or isolated. Those subjects to which we have
applied ourselves seem almost as part of us, but those
to which our inclination and earlier education have not
led us, tend to appear as strange and beyond our power
to grasp. We are apt to get a fixed idea that it is impossible for us to acquire such branches of knowledge
or skill. As, however, "Nihil humani a me alienum
puto" is a fine saying in relation to morality, so it
also has meaning in regard to technical acquirement;
but its full significance is only to be sought for in the
realm of knowledge.

An educated man has not really narrowed his nature,
but rather made it capable of everything. In order to
acquire fresh knowledge and skill, nothing more is
needed than that he shall take the matter in hand and
grapple with it straight, instead of standing appalled
at the idea of possible difficulties, or dreading that
he may prove incompetent.

Now military exercises used to be considered as very
incompatible with study; but in truth they are neither
unsuitable nor devoid of interest for youth at this stage.
Perhaps the chief value, however, of the experiment
of introducing them into the school is in destroying any
notion of a barrier erected to separate our work from
the life of the world. These exercises may also serve
a still higher purpose by reminding the pupils of the
possibility that each, whatever his rank or work in life,

may be called upon to defend his country, or at least to help in preparing for such defence. This is a natural duty, formerly realised by all citizens, but to which gradually whole ranks of society have become strangers.

IV. The Necessary Balance between Receptivity and Self-Activity

(*Extract from Second Address*)

To regard study as mere receptivity and memory work is to have a most incomplete view of what instruction really means. On the other hand, to concentrate attention on the pupil's own original reflections and reasoning is equally one-sided and should be still more carefully guarded against.

The pupils of Pythagoras were compelled to be silent during the first four years under instruction, that is, they were neither to have nor to express any original ideas and thoughts. It is an essential aim of education to eradicate those merely personal ideas, thoughts and reflections which are specially characteristic of youth. Like the will, thought must begin with obedience.

But if learning limited itself to mere *receiving*, the effect would not be much better than if we wrote sentences on water : for it is not the receiving but the self-activity of comprehension and the power to use it again, that first makes knowledge our own possession.

If the direction is reversed, so as first to emphasise the pupil's own reasoning, there will be neither training nor order in thought, no connection and no sequence in knowledge.

In order to receive, however, personal effort is needful, not in the form of original thought, but as application of what has been learnt, as endeavour to bring it into right relation with other particular cases and other concrete examples.

The nature of what is taught in school, from the first grammatical definition onward, is not a series of isolated sense phenomena, of which each is only of value in itself, and merely an object of observation, of imagination, or of memory ; but it is rather a series of rules, general concepts, thoughts and laws.

V. THE RELATION OF THE SCHOOL AND SCHOOL INSTRUCTION TO THE GENERAL MORAL EDUCATION OF MANKIND

(*Extract from Third Address*)

On the nature of this relation depends the significance and value of many arrangements and methods of procedure adopted in the school. Since the discipline and moral activity of the school cannot extend to the whole company of the pupil's daily life, because this whole compass is not entrusted to it, so its activity is to some extent limited by this fact. But, on the other hand, it is just this sharp limitation that gives to the school its special function, and defines its proper sphere of influence.

We are so accustomed to regard that as alone effective which has a direct bearing on the end in view, that we tend to expect moral effects to follow only from direct moral instruction, discipline and example. But the indirect influence which is due to instruction in arts and sciences must not be lost sight of.

There is another and still more important aspect of influence in regard to the formation of moral principles and conduct, which falls to the duty of the school—that, namely, according to which principles and modes of conduct are not brought to the conscious reflection of the mind, but become rather a vital atmosphere, in which the human being lives and to which his mental life becomes accustomed and adapted, so that, under its influence, right principles appear to him in the form of common practice and tend to become habitual.

That which concerns the first of these—direct instruction in moral ideas and principles—forms an essential part of our school curriculum. Also such ideas, instruction and examples are incidentally contained in the teaching material (*i.e.* books), in the use of which the pupils are exercised in learning languages.

One may become impatient of the endless talk about morality which, for many reasons, is now heard on all sides, and be led to consider definite moral teaching as superfluous, largely because in all this sage discourse about the subject, evil passions, little irritations and especially moral self-conceit tend to come to the fore. But all this makes it none the less true and important for us to remember that it is not enough to rely entirely on the natural development of good in the heart and on the habituation to right living by means of example, without the aid of reflection.

We must make the conscious mind acquainted with

moral ends, strengthen in it moral resolutions and lead it to reflection upon them. For in these moral ideas we have the bases and standpoints from which we can justify our actions—the guiding lines which lead us through the complexities of appearance and the uncertain play of the feelings.

It is the advantage of self-conscious reflection that, instead of the fixity of animal instinct, it is quite free in choosing its own ends, and yet of its own free will sets limits to itself.

Firmness and restraint, as opposed to instability and inconsistency, are the necessary moral, and still more, religious ends to be secured. Failing such, man neglects what is for the common good of mankind, and chooses that which happens to appeal to him at the moment.

It is one of the prejudices which has become widespread in modern times through the " Enlightenment " (which has too often led to the exchange of good old customs and fundamental principles—because they were not really understood—for those which are superficial, worthless, even harmful) that youth must neither be taught moral ideas and principles, nor even be given religious instruction in early years, because such teaching cannot be understood and only resolves itself into committing words to memory. But, on more careful consideration, it is easy to observe that ideas relating to moral practice can be well understood by the child, the boy and the youth, in such measure as their respective ages allow.

Indeed our whole life is nothing more than an endeavour to understand, ever more completely, their meaning and extent, to see them reflected in new and ever

newer examples and instances, and only thus to recog-
nise more clearly their full meaning and exact application.   Indeed, if it were necessary to wait until one
was completely capable of grasping the full import
of these practical moral ideas, few would ever possess
this power, and these few hardly before the end of their
lives.   It would be the lack of exercise of moral reflection itself, as well as that of right moral feelings, which
would delay the growth of this power of understanding.
It is here the same as with other kinds of ideas and
concepts, the understanding of which begins in like
manner, with knowledge not fully understood.   That a
general alone should be allowed to know the word
" battle," because only he knows actually what it is—
would be an example of the same kind of demand.

But it is not only a question of right understanding.
Moral ideas and their modes of expression ought to become rooted in the soul, and to attain this end they must
be impressed early.   They include within themselves
the main outlines and foundations of an inner, higher
world.   Fixed in youth, they form a treasure which has
life in itself, which grows, increases and is enriched by
experience, and assures to itself ever more insight and
certainty.

Further, also, formal training in regard to moral
conduct is necessary, because such conduct implies ability to apprehend rightly situations and circumstances,
to distinguish clearly between the moral ends in question,
and to make the best use of them.   Now, it is precisely
this ability which is developed through systematic instruction ; for this exercises the sense of relativity and is a

sure path to facility in distinguishing the particular from the general, and conversely, the application of the general to the particular.

Above all, systematic training has the effect of detaching the mind from itself, from its immediate natural existence, of raising it from the narrow sphere of feeling and impulse, and of giving it freedom in the sphere of thought. Thereby it attains a higher consciousness than that of the merely necessary reaction upon external impressions ; and through this enfranchisement comes power to deal with immediate presentations and experiences. The formal ideas which lie at the root of moral conduct are of special value in promoting this enfranchisement.

The school does not, however, stop short at these general effects ; it is also a special moral condition in which man sojourns for a while, and in which he is morally trained through becoming habituated to actual circumstances. It is a sphere which has its own content and affairs, its own justice and laws, its punishments and rewards, and it is indeed a sphere which constitutes an essential stage in the formation of complete moral character.

VI. The Relation Between the School and the Family

(Extract from Third Address)

The school stands between the family and the real world, and forms the connecting link in the transition from one to the other.

Life in the family, which precedes life in the school, is a personal relation, one of feeling, of love, of natural faith and trust ; it is not a business tie or compact, but the natural bond of blood.   The child is of value because he is the child.   He receives the love of his parents, without merit on his part ; so also he has to endure their anger without the right to resent it.

On the contrary, in the world man is only valued on account of what he does, he has merit only in so far as he earns it.   He will receive little from love and for love's sake ; here the deed alone counts, not the sentiment and the individual person concerned.   The world con- stitutes a community independent of the conscious individual mind.   Therein a man is of value, according to his skill and usefulness in one of its spheres of action, which value is greater the more he rids himself of his personal peculiarities and develops a sense of universal life and action.

The school is the intermediate stage which leads man from the family circle out into the world ; removes him from his natural inner world of feeling and inclination, and places him in the external realm of things and deeds·

This is to say, that in the school the activity of the child begins first to have serious meaning, so that it is no longer subject to caprice and chance, to momentary pleasure and inclination.   The child learns to regulate his actions according to rules and with regard to some aim in view.   He ceases to be valued only for himself, and begins to be of worth for what he does and to earn his own reputation.

In the family the child has to do right in the sense

of rendering personal obedience and love ; in the school
he has to behave according to a sense of duty and of law,
and to do these and to leave undone other things (which
may formerly have been permissible to him as an
individual) in the interest of general, and perhaps merely
formal, order.

Taught in common with many others, he learns to
adjust himself to others, to acquire trust in people
almost strangers to him, confidence in himself in reference to them ; and thereby begins the formation and
practice of the social virtues.

There begins now for the human being the double
existence into which his life generally divides, and between
the ever-increasing extremes of which he must, for the
future, maintain the balance. The first unity and
completeness of his natural life conditions disappears ;
he now belongs to two distinct spheres of action, each of
which lays claim to one side of his life alone. Apart
from what the school requires from him, he has one side
of life left free from its control ; this side is partly subject
to home requirements, but is partly also left to his own
choice and direction. Thus he has at once a side of
his life no longer merely conditioned by the family,
and also a kind of independent existence with special
duties of its own.

One other of the results which follow from the consideration of the nature of this manner of life concerns the tone, the external organisation, also all
that is included under the term discipline, as carried
out in such an institution as ours. The views as to what
is meant by discipline, and especially school discipline,

have altered greatly during the progress of civilisation. Since education is coming more and more to be regarded from the right standpoint, that is, that it must be in its essence rather support and encouragement, than suppression of the awakening consciousness—a training to independent life and power—it has ceased to be the custom in the family, as in the school, to induce in children a feeling of subjection and bondage—to make them obey another's will even in unimportant matters— to demand absolute obedience for obedience' sake, and by severity to obtain what really belongs alone to the feeling of love and reverence and the grave issues of the case in question.

We must require from the pupils in our school quiet and attention during lessons ; polite behaviour towards their teachers and fellow-pupils ; the performance of allotted tasks ; and, above all, that obedience which is needful for the attainment of those ends towards which their studies are directed. But at the same time it is understood that conduct, in regard to indifferent matters— those which do not concern the order of the school—is to be left entirely free. In the intercourse of study, in an association of which the bond and interest are to be found in knowledge and intellectual activity—lack of freedom is peculiarly inappropriate. A society of students cannot be regarded as an assemblage of servants, nor should they have the appearance or behaviour of such. Education to independence demands that young people should be accustomed early to consult their own sense of propriety and their own reason ; that a free sphere of action should be left to them, in which they can

determine their own conduct to each other and in relation
to older people.

In addition to this necessary freedom, there also
follows from the foregoing the question of the limitation
of the area over which the school can exercise its
discipline. The pupil has only one foot in the school,
and inasmuch as the responsibility for his private conduct does not rest with it alone, the teachers cannot be
held responsible by the public for any special acts or
behaviour of the pupil outside the school and school hours.
Not only are the pupils, for the greater part of their
time, under other powerful influences, so that the school
must content itself with the general efficacy of its work,
as previously indicated, but it must specially be remembered that once outside the school they again come
under the control of their parents or guardians. It is
for these latter to determine what freedom their children
shall have, what society shall be allowed them, and what
shall be their expenditure and their amusements. When
the behaviour of the pupils is found to be blame-
worthy, it may be said on the one hand: They are pupils
of such and such school who behave in this way; or on
the other hand it may be said : They are the children
of those parents—the sons of the present age ! To be
just in judgment, we must consider which aspect is the
true one in any particular case.

Thus the school shares with the family in the life of
the young. It is in the highest degree needful that they
should not obstruct each other, that one should not
weaken the authority and respect of the other, but
that they should rather afford mutual support, and

work together to attain their important and common aims.

On the other side the school has a relation to the wider world of action for which it is its business to prepare the young. This wider world appears as a firm, consistent whole of laws and regulations directed towards the public welfare, in which individuals are of value only in so far as they conform and contribute to this end. It does not concern itself about their special aims, intentions and modes of thought. Into this system of universality, however, there are woven likewise—personal inclinations, individual passions and the impelling force of material interests. The world displays the drama of the conflict between these two sides.

In the school private interests and selfish passions are silent, it is a sphere of work mainly concerned with ideas and thoughts. If, however, school life is passionless, it is on that account too, lacking in the higher interest and seriousness of public life ; it is only a silent, inward preparation and equipment for it. What the school really tries to accomplish in the education of individuals is to make them fit to take part in public life. The knowledge and skill which are acquired first attain their true end and aim in application to affairs which take place outside the school.

Further, knowledge and skill only come under consideration in the school in so far as they can be acquired by the pupils. Knowledge itself will not be advanced or extended, but only acquired by study in the form in which it is already within reach and even then in its elements alone.

M

School studies consist in that which has long been common knowledge. School tasks have no complete end in themselves ; they only lay the foundations for and make possible the real work of life. If, however, the content of the school studies consists of that which has long been known and accepted, the individual pupils, who are now first being educated by its means, are in no sense complete or finished when it has been acquired by them. This preparation work, which we call education—does not perfect, but only secures a step in advance.

Now as that which takes place in the family circle has its chief interest and value within the same, in so far at least as it concerns the value and interest of individuals alone ; so school work, its verdicts, its distinctions and its punishments have also in the main but a relative importance and find their chief validity within this school sphere. In school youth is in the act of striving. He who lags behind has still before him the general possibility of improvement ; the possibility that he has not yet found his own proper standpoint and interest, or that he has not yet reached his " moment " of intellectual awakening.[1]

On the other hand, sometimes a pupil distinguishes himself at first and makes quick progress in the early stages of work, but falls behind when the demand comes for deeper study. He resembles the rock upon which the seed fell and at first grew up quickly, but soon

[1] *Cf.* the passage in Wordsworth's Prelude :
"Such glory was but little sought by me,
   And little won . . .
              I was not for that hour,
   Nor for that place."

withered. Then again another appears for a long time
as an unopened kernel, slow to apprehend and to make
progress, but who, however, stores everything deeply,
lets it take root in his mind and then quite suddenly
attains to power and ease of expression.

On this account the judgment passed by the school
(*i.e.* on any pupil) can as little be regarded as final as
the human being can be called perfect. It has therefore been enacted, first, that the criticisms made on
the pupil's work should not be publicly announced;
secondly, that it shall be expressly stated, when they
are read aloud to the pupils, that they are to be regarded
as the free views of their teachers, but that these have no
direct influence on the future profession of any pupil
or on the position he may come to occupy in the world.

For, as the work of the school is of the nature of
practice and preparation, so also is its verdict one given
in advance, and however important an opinion it represents, it can by no means be regarded as final. Pro-
motions in class or to higher classes at the end of the
school year are public, but indeed only very general
verdicts on what each pupil has accomplished. The
uncertainty which reigns in this world of becoming shows
itself strikingly in this connection.

VII. The Nature of the Connection between School Studies and Professional Knowledge

(Extract from Fourth Address)

In the classics, the study of which has the chief place
in the school (gymnasium) curriculum, are found the

beginnings and fundamental conceptions of knowledge, or, generally speaking, of what is worth knowing, and they are therefore specially suitable as preparation for professional studies, while in relation to the fine arts, they may be regarded as the consummation. They are specially distinguished by this characteristic—that in them abstract reflections still remain close to the concrete, and that concepts are ever built up from examples. Presentations of human affairs in their reality form the bases; and are here set forth together with the general results and inferences which follow from them. Abstract thought has thus a living freshness; we receive it in its simplicity, united with the personal feeling and individuality of the conditions from which it arose ; it has on this account singular clearness and intelligibility.

As the form has this concrete completeness, so has also the content ; and it concerns human, and especially public, life directly. That which, through the organisation of modern times, has been removed from our observation and our sympathy—the passions, the deeds and the struggles of nations—the great underlying circumstances which result in the union of that civil and moral order on which rest the life of states, the position, interest and activity of individuals—are brought vividly before our eyes.

The classical period stands in the happy mean between the crude simplicity of a nation in its ignorant childhood and the refined intellect and judgment of the civilisation which has analysed and specialised everything. In this latter case the inner life of the whole is as an abstract spirit, far withdrawn from the mind of the individual ; each one receives but a dismembered and isolated share thereof, limited to a confined sphere, above which the real soul of the world lives and watches, taking account of all those wheels and separate motions, and leading ever towards unity ; but the individuals experience neither the feeling nor the active presentation of the whole.

As we generally devote ourselves to some special profession, we occupy a position removed from any possible view of the whole, we assign to ourselves but a narrow sphere of life.   The ideals of youth are boundless ; reality is spoken of as sad, because it does not correspond to that infinity.   But all effective life, activity and character have this essential condition in common : that of concentration upon some definite aim.   He who will do great things, says the poet, must be able to set limits to himself.[1]

The profession or station in life to which we devote ourselves is, however, more exclusive in our time than it was with the ancients.   In any given calling we lose the life of the whole in a wider sense than was the case in their time.   So much the more important is it for us— just because we are human, and because we are reasonable beings established on the basis of the eternal and the ideal—to develop and hold fast in ourselves the vision and the concept of complete living.   To this idea classical studies specially lead us.   The classics give the most intimate presentation of the whole circle of human life ; the nature and mode of the freedom to be found in the

[1] Goethe's lines :
    "Wer Grosses will, muss sich zusammenraffen," etc.

ancient states, the close connection of public and private life, of general thought and personal opinion, make it possible to present the great interests of individual humanity, the mightiest pillars of public and of private activity, the powers which overthrow and raise up nations—as ideas belonging to a continuous circle of thought, as simple, natural observations of everyday occurences in a familiar present—ideas which in our state of civilisation do not enter into the circle of our life and activity. In this way also laws and duties appear to us in living form as moral customs and virtues ; not as reflections and principles according to which we must regulate our actions as by remote and prescribed precepts.

It is at the university that the further separation begins, the closer application to the special calling or profession, yet do not forget your school studies. Do not forget them because of their usefulness as means to further knowledge ; but also for this reason, that you may retain ever present to your minds the ideas on which a noble life is based, and that you may keep for yourselves an inner region of beauty to which you will gladly retreat from the isolation of life in the world, but from which also you can return to your profession and settled activity, strengthened and refreshed, free from the weariness of longing, or the idle weakness of reverie.

VIII. STUDY AND CHARACTER-BUILDING

(Extract from Fifth Address)

Study in the quiet seclusion of the school is the best and most suitable way of giving the young interest and employment, which will keep them from the stir and excitement and the seductive influences of the fermenting condition of our time.

There must now be redoubled care on the part of parents and guardians to watch over and to protect those committed to their charge. It is difficult to find the middle course in dealing with children, between too great freedom and too great restriction. If kind-hearted parents gladly allow an innocent freedom to their children, yet care must be taken to secure that it truly is, and remains, innocent. Since it is easier to love children than to train them, parents must be quite certain that it is not indolence on their part if they leave their sons to themselves, instead of keeping them under supervision and guiding them assiduously. The principle that it is good to bring children early into contact with the world has done much harm in modern education. This implies leading them to take part in the pleasures and distractions of grown-up people, without first securing that they are prepared to participate in them with safety. Experience shows that this is a mistake. Rather is it found that men who have had a good grounding in moral ideas and have also been trained in good manners and conduct, soon learn how to assume the required customs of outward appearance and

behaviour when they go out into the world. Some of
the most distinguished men of the world have come
forth from the narrow life of the cloister. On the other
hand, men who have been brought up in the midst of
worldly superficiality never attain the true inwardness
of life.

But little reflection is needed in order to realise this.
The inner foundation of character must be made strong
and firm, if true ability and capacity for work are to
result. The danger is that the young, seeing only the
glitter of outward life and the apparent importance with
which it is treated by men to whose opinion they attach
authority and significance, may consider this aspect as
the whole, or at least the only important side of life,
because they do not at the same time learn to know the
really solid and serious business which these persons
pursue apart from such recreation. Thus the young
receive a false idea of value and give themselves up to
this excitement, which is attained without effort and is
bound up with so much pleasure.

They learn to despise, and at the same time to shirk,
all those virtues which are esteemed, and regarded as
duties, in the school. But there is another danger
which lies in wait for the young, one more closely connected with study itself. The greatness and importance
of the subjects studied and the consequent awakening
in the mind of the sense of their true value for life, may
lead the young to an imaginary idea of their own
maturity and to the assumption of the independent
behaviour of grown-up people, and of an equality in
their pleasures and outward manner of life. How-

ever well parents may be pleased with what their sons have done, and however great the confidence they may have in them, it is yet important neither to let them have the reins in their own hands, nor to consider further care and discipline as unnecessary. Such freedom, allowed through over-confidence, brings with it the danger of falling into folly and bad habits, and even into dissoluteness and crime.

Let us parents and teachers mutually support each other in carrying out the aims of the moral education of our boys. By means of this alliance we may hope to see our work—of training them to be strong, capable and moral men—crowned with success.

It is specially reserved for the rising generation to reap the fruits of the good which is now issuing and which will still continue to unfold itself from so many years of confusion and trouble. May they and we with them leave the storms of this weary time behind. Thus they may be able—untroubled by memory of losses suffered —of other habits and modes of thought—to grasp with youthful freshness the new form of life which we have seen arise and to whose riper development we look forward in anticipation.

A great epoch has been born in the world. May you, boys, prepare yourselves worthily for it—ensure the greater ability which its service demands, and win also the happiness which shall result from its unfolding.

IX. School Organisation

Extract from Niethammer's " Normativ," or " General Code of Regulations for the Public Educational Institutions in the Kingdom of Bavaria " [1]

This educational institution (Studiensanstalt) consists
1. of a lower and upper primary school, each of which has again two divisions, so that each pupil must spend therein at least four years.
2. The primary school leads on to the Progymnasium, which has a two-year course of study.
3. After that follows the Gymnasium proper, in which in four years the pupils pass through four classes— namely, the lower class, the lower and upper middle classes, and, finally, the Gymnasial class itself.

As regards curriculum, the chief subjects of study (and rightly so) which will occupy the attention of the pupils are the classical languages. For in regard to training value, precision, flexibility and richness, the classical languages are the most perfect, and (as every living language is subject to continual change) the best means of effectively developing good taste and of training the intellect and heart of studious youth.

There is no kind of beautiful literature in which the Greeks and Romans have not accomplished something

---

[1] This extract deals only with the type of educational institution known as the Gymnasium. In this connection, " Primary School " is really the equivalent of Preparatory School, leading on to the Gymnasium, or Secondary School proper. " Primar- schule " must not be confounded with " Volksschule," which is more nearly the equivalent of our term " Elementary School."

excellent.   In their writings we find the greatest masterpieces of rhetorical art, poetry and eloquence.   In these
we are enchanted with the most beautiful pictures, the
great deeds of their heroes and the marvellous wisdom
of their statesmen.   There is stored the greatest treasure
of human knowledge and experience.   In these writings
are to be found the finest, sublimest ideas expressed in
the most musical and most perfect language.   Even
in their philosophical works a lofty, yet simple, spirit
reigns, a clear, living presentation, for the most part far
removed alike from subtlety and from aridity.

The Greeks and the Romans understood the art—
so helpful in its bearing on life—of recognising things
as they really are.   In observation they knew how to
make clear distinctions, and to clothe the results achieved
by their ever active intellects in beautiful forms of expression, perfectly suited to the nature of the subject
treated.   In one word—they had made their own the
sublime art of finding truth and of giving it fit expression.

As the influence of the Greek and Roman classics has
such a beneficial effect on the education of the young,
as the treasures which the poet, the orator, the historian,
the philosopher and the statesman derive from them are
so valuable, it cannot appear strange to anyone that
pupils in each primary school, and even in the first
school year, should (in addition to German instruction)
devote *ten* hours weekly to Latin, in order that they may
obtain the necessary grammatical preparation to enable
them to translate, without mistakes, selected extracts
suitable to their age—from German into Latin, or from
Latin into German.

In the Progymnasium, where the study of Greek is introduced with *seven* hours, and *six* hours weekly are devoted to instruction in Latin, the pupils should receive such preparation that they may attain for themselves readiness in regard to the technique of the two languages, together with an adequate store of words, so that on entering the Gymnasium proper they may not be hindered from making the acquaintance of the best Greek and Roman classics. Then through examination and analysis of the fundamental rules that have been stated they may make their powers of judgment more acute, correct their concepts, exercise their ingenuity and power of penetration, so that in them may awaken inclination and love for what is true, great and noble. And in order that this aim may be more surely attained, *two* hours a week are set apart in the lower middle class for the study of Greek and Roman Mythology and Antiquities, whereby the pupil receives instruction and necessary aids for the right understanding of Greek and Roman authors.

Since France has also produced masterpieces of wit and learning, and as the circumstances of the time have united us in close bonds with this great nation, the French language has also become a subject of public instruction, which begins in the upper primary school with *three* hours per week, and is continued on up to the higher Gymnasial class.

In addition to the study of languages, other subjects are also taught which are not only selected in view of the training of the intellect, but are such as have also bearing and influence on the heart. Amongst these religious instruction merits, doubtless, the first place.

If the young are carefully trained in the Christian religion, instructed in the content of this divine teaching in a manner suitable to their age and powers of comprehension; if this religion and its divine founder are presented to them as worthy of admiration and love; if they are led to model their characters on that of the founder, encouraged to close observation of his commands and to eager imitation of his example, there will be kindled within their minds that sure light, lacking which, man still wanders in darkness. It will awake in them a keen sense of right and wrong; a feeling for truth, goodness and beauty. It will afford them peace of heart, courage and strength for good works, consolation in suffering and hope for the future.

For the purpose of this branch of study, the most important and most sacred of mankind, *three* hours weekly will be required in the lower and upper primary schools; in the Progymnasium, *two*, and in the lower Gymnasial class, in which knowledge of rights and duties is combined with religious teaching, *four* teaching hours.

If the teaching of history is properly carried on, so that the inner motives of human actions are sought out; the causes and results considered in their relation to each other, and facts estimated in their true proportions; then the pupil receives not merely training in orderly thought, but also obtains the richest profit for his heart. It teaches him by the experience of centuries what evil sin has brought upon the earth, how the decline of morals has been the forerunner and the cause of the fall of nations, as of individuals. History holds up to youth great examples for imitation and admiration and shows him the ways of divine providence. This important subject is to be pursued in the upper primary school and in the higher classes of the Progymnasium as a course of general history for *four* hours per week, and in the two higher classes of the Gymnasium itself, a course in some special period, also for *four* hours per week. In order, however, that human actions may be rightly judged, it is necessary to be acquainted with the earthly stage upon which the human race makes its appearance. In regard to this, Geography, a knowledge of which is also presupposed in whatever step one may take in the service of Church and State, or as a citizen of the world, is laid down as a necessary subject and is to be taught in the lower primary school for *four* hours, in the first course of the Progymnasium for *three* hours, and in the lower Gymnasial classes for *two* hours per week.

The study of Mathematics gives to the intellect readiness in thinking correctly and deeply, and if happily these characteristics are shared by the soul, then it is in a good position to choose and to act constantly according to the clear insight of reason. This branch of knowledge also forms a subject of instruction for all classes in this institution and is taught for *three* hours per week in the primary schools, the Progymnasium and in the lower middle class of the Gymnasium, and in the remaining classes for *four* hours weekly.

The branches of knowledge which furnish us with information about the visible world, the great and marvellous works of the eternal architect, are those which make us acquainted with the earth beneath, impart instruction in regard to the things therein to be found, their nature, value and utility, or teach us to raise our thought to the starry heavens and the countless worlds above us.   These studies will not only correct our ideas and clear our understanding, but also tune our heart to inmost feelings of gratitude, and transport us with deepest reverence and adoration.

These include Physiography and Cosmography, for the first of which *two* hours of weekly instruction are arranged for in the upper middle class, and for the latter *three* hours per week in the lower middle class.

Once the pupils have had made known to them the methods of orderly and correct thinking, an introductory survey of the whole scheme of the philosophical sciences should be given to them.   If in this the most important truths are set forth in their interconnection, and each of these truths based upon such evidence as is within the pupil's powers of comprehension, then they will not only more easily apprehend the more complete instruction in Philosophy given in academic lectures, but they will turn this knowledge to useful account in the direction of their activity.   For the more skilful one is in distinguishing between truth and error according to reliable rules, the more one learns to know the properties of things, of the world and of its author, the less is one likely to speak of these in a confident way and lightly, according to personal inclination and impression, still less to allow oneself to be robbed of the conviction concerning one's duties by means of sophistical reasoning.

In order to secure to the pupils this advantage in their studies, *four* hours a week are given in the Gymnasial classes to instruction in Logic and Metaphysics, and those objects of speculative thought which were formerly dealt with separately are united together in a philosophical encyclopædia.

In addition to the subjects so far considered, which have in view the enlightenment of the understanding and the cultivation of the heart—technical arts (*i.e.* writing, drawing, etc.) are also given place as branches of instruction, and so the pupils in the lower primary school are exercised in the art of penmanship for *six* hours, in the upper primary school for *three* hours, and the pupils in the Progymnasium in penmanship and drawing for *six* hours weekly.

These are the prescribed subjects of study in the general regulations. As regards the amount of time to be given to instruction, there are prescribed *thirty-two* teaching hours in each of the two primary schools and each course of the Progymnasium and *twenty-seven* hours for each class in the Gymnasium itself.